ADVENTURES

IN THE

RIFLE BRIGADE

IN THE

PENINSULA

FRANCE AND THE NETHERLANDS

FROM 1809 TO 1815

ADVENTURES

IN THE

RIFLE BRIGADE

IN THE PENINSULA, FRANCE AND THE
NETHERLANDS FROM 1809 TO 1815

BY

CAPTAIN JOHN KINCAID

The Spellmount Library of Military History

SPELLMOUNT
Staplehurst

British Library Cataloguing in Publication Data:
A catalogue record for this book is available
from the British Library

Copyright © Spellmount 1998
Introduction © Ian Fletcher 1998

ISBN 1-86227-020-1

First published in 1830

This edition first published in the UK in 1998
in
The Spellmount Library of Military History
by
Spellmount Limited
The Old Rectory
Staplehurst
Kent TN12 0AZ

1 3 5 7 9 8 6 4 2

Printed in Great Britain by
T.J. International Ltd
Padstow, Cornwall

AN INTRODUCTION
By Ian Fletcher

'One day's trench-work is as like another as the days themselves; and like nothing better than serving an apprenticeship to the double calling of grave-digger and gamekeeper, for we found ample employment both for the spade and shovel.' So wrote Captain John Kincaid, of the 95th Rifles, during the siege of Badajoz in March and April 1812. There were not many men who could make light of their lot before the walls of Badajoz but then again there were not too many men of the calibre of Kincaid, a man whose exploits in the Peninsula and at Waterloo form probably the most famous of the many memoirs written by men who took part in these two great campaigns. Of course, you had to have survived to have taken such a whimsical view of events in the Peninsula, but survive he did, and in some style.

John Kincaid, a Scot, and the son of a farmer, joined the 95th Rifles at the age of 22, attracted by the glamorous green uniform and by the nature of its services and achievements. 'Hurrah for the first in the field and the last out of it, the fighting ninety-fifth', was cry of the day that attracted so many young men to the ranks of the green-jacketed riflemen. It is no coincidence that the reasons for which Kincaid joined the 95th account for its widespread appeal today and its reputation as the most famous of Wellington's regiments. They fired, in Kincaid's words, 'the first and last shot in almost every battle, siege and skirmish in which the Army was engaged during the war.' Indeed, the regiment fired the first British shots of the war, at Brillos, on August 16th 1808, and suffered the first officer casualty of the war during the same skirmish. This amounted to a vast amount of expended lead, for the 95th took part in nearly all of the great battles and sieges between 1808 and 1815, from Rolica to Waterloo.

It was also one of the most progressive regiments in the British army in terms of training and discipline, being one of the regiments of light infantry trained by Sir John Moore at Shorncliffe. In the hands of Coote Manningham and William Stewart, the 95th quickly established its own individuality. Great emphasis was placed on internal discipline, good marksmanship and on keeping things simple. As Kincaid himself wrote, 'the beauty of their system of discipline consisted in their doing everything that was necessary and nothing that was not, so that every man's duty was a pleasure to him, and the esprit de corps was unrivalled.' The end result was the formation of a superb fighting elite with tremendous regimental spirit. It is probably for this reason that Bernard Cornwell chose the 95th as the home for Richard Sharpe and his sidekicks, Harper, Hagman and Harris, the heroes in his best-selling Sharpe novels.

The weapon used by the 95th, the famous Baker rifle, is another reason for the enduring fame of the regiment, it being used by no other British regiment except the 5/60th. During the long years of the war in Portugal and Spain, the accuracy and reliability of the rifle proved more than a match for the skirmishers of the French army and gave Wellington a very distinct advantage on many occasions. In the hands of a trained rifleman the Baker proved a superb weapon, slow to load and fire but deadly when the trigger was finally pulled. Being an officer, of course, Kincaid would rarely have picked up the rifle, if at all, but we do know that in some regiments the officers were the best shots and we find the private soldiers loading the faithful India pattern muskets for their officers. It is the stuff of Hollywood, of course, but it did happen. William Thornton Keep, of the 28th, was one of two officers wounded whilst acting in a skirmishing role during the battle of

St Pierre, on December 13th 1813. We know also that groups of Guards' officers formed shooting parties during the siege of the Salamanca/Burgos forts, probably using their own privately purchased firearms. It is highly likely, therefore, that even the officers of the 95th used the Baker on occasion.

The high standard of education of the 95th's officers, and, in fact, its men, is reflected in the number of quality memoirs written by them. Amongst their number we find the accounts by George Simmons, William Surtees, Harry Smith and Jonathan Leach (all classics), and Robert Fernyhough, whilst Jonathan Green and Edward Costello, two more classics, are amongst those written by ordinary riflemen. Each of these memoirs gives us a wonderful account of life in Wellington's army but none has the humour which Kincaid introduces us to in his. The timing of Kincaid's *Adventures*, 1830, is also worthy of mention, coming two years after the publication of the first volume of Napier's great magnum opus, *The History of the War in the Peninsula*. It is, therefore, free from any of Napier's influence, something which pervades many a Peninsular memoir. Napier, in fact, acts as a nice companion to Kincaid, and provides valuable historical background, he himself serving in the Light Division with Kincaid, albeit with the 43rd. He was, therefore, privy at close quarters to many of the events in which Kincaid participated. Kincaid's follow-up, *Random Shots from a Rifleman*, was published in 1835 and is also almost entirely free of any Napier, containing many of the humorous anecdotes omitted from *Adventures*.

Another reason for the 95th's fame is that it formed part of the famous Light Brigade, later the Light Division, alongside the 43rd and 52nd Light Infantry regiments, and the 1st and 3rd Portuguese Caçadores. Place the division under the command of probably the most controversial and charismatic commander in Wellington's army, Robert 'Black Bob' Craufurd, and you have a very potent cocktail. On several occasions, you had merely to light the blue touch-paper and stand back. The golden years of the division really occurred between 1809 and 1812 when Craufurd led his men both to glory and to controversy. The famous march to Talavera, which saw the then Light Brigade cover over 40 miles in just 25 hours but arrive too late to take part in the battle, perhaps typifies the division's story under Black Bob, brilliance tinged with disappointment and, on occasion, with mistake. Indeed, the battles of Busaco, Sabugal and Fuentes de Oñoro, and the storming of Ciudad Rodrigo can be offset by the mishaps at the Coa river and at Barquilla. None of these latter affairs could be laid at the feet of the regiments themselves for it was Craufurd who blundered on these occasions and, indeed, it was only the skill of the regimental commanders during the action on the Coa that extricated the Light Division from a potentially disastrous situation. But at Busaco, and during the operations on the Coa and Agueda rivers during the spring and summer of 1810 – the Coa and Barquilla excepted – Craufurd and his men were simply superb. Even Sir Charles Oman, the great historian of the Peninsular War, was moved to write of this latter operation that, so successful was Craufurd's chain of outposts, 'the whole web of communications quivered at the slightest touch.' After the fight at Barba del Puerco, on March 19th 1810, even Wellington was moved to write about the action to Admiral Berkeley, declaring that the French were 'repulsed in fine style'.

When Craufurd was mortally wounded leading the Light Division into the Lesser Breach at Ciudad Rodrigo on January 19th 1812, the flare with which the division had fought died with him. The Light Division was never quite the same under its subsequent commanders, such as Charles Alten, but many of its, and the 95th's, finest achievements were achieved between 1812 and the end of the war, particularly when Wellington's army entered the

Pyrenees and the area of the Nivelle and the Nive, where the 95th found itself in its element. Indeed, the triangle between Bayonne, the Nive and the Atlantic, where the rolling hills, rivers and rugged countryside made normal tactical operations difficult, was made for the men of the 95th, their green jackets and extended open order of fighting proving invaluable. It is a great shame that Wellington was bereft of the Light Division when he fought Napoleon at Waterloo in June 1815. Kincaid was there with the 95th, as was the 52nd Light Infantry. Sadly, the 43rd, hurrying back from America, landed at Ostend on June 18th, the very day of the great battle, and so missed fighting alongside its comrades of the old Light Division.

John Kincaid entered the pages of history not in the Peninsula, but at the fever-ridden island of Walcheren in the summer of 1809. In January of that year, the 1st Battalion of the 95th had returned to England following the harrowing Corunna campaign. The men returned to their barracks at Hythe in a terrible condition and upon arrival simply piled up what was left of their ragged uniforms and made a large bonfire of them. Six months later the Rifles were off again, this time the 2nd Battalion, bound for Walcheren. Kincaid was among them but he wrote nothing about his experiences there in his *Adventures* nor in his *Random Shots*. Suffice to say that it was a thoroughly unpleasant and ill-fated venture.

After this false start, Kincaid returned to England but in September of 1810 was overseas again, this time in Portugal where he joined his battalion as it was making its way south to the Lines of Torres Vedras. It was the start of a long adventure that was to take him from Lisbon, into Spain, over the Pyrenees and into France, and finally to the field of Waterloo. During all of his service, he was fortunate to be wounded only once, at Foz d'Arouce on March 13th 1811, during Massena's retreat to Spain. Along the way Kincaid witnessed some of the bloodiest battles in the Peninsula, none more so than at the storming of Badajoz on the night of April 6th 1812. In this passage, he demonstrates why he is such a superb writer, his vivid description of the storming, his lapse into a passage of respectful seriousness, and yet returning afterwards to his humorous, jaunty style.

For all of his lightheartedness, Kincaid provides us with an insight into some of the British army's great personalities, such as Craufurd, Beckwith and Wellington himself. Craufurd was never loved by his men and, in fact, was positively loathed by some officers of the 95th. But when all was said and done, and when the Light Division had buried its leader, his coffin borne by six battle-hardened but tearful veterans, Kincaid was moved to write that Craufurd, 'was better known than liked, but like many a gem of purer ray his value was scarcely known until lost.' He reserved nothing but the utmost respect and praise for Sydney Beckwith, who led the 95th to so much glory until ill-health forced him from the game in April 1812, while Wellington receives equal praise. In fact, Kincaid wrote, 'that I never should have forgiven the Frenchman that had killed me before I effected it,' that is, before he had lain eyes on the great man.

One of Kincaid's most memorable episodes came after the storming of Badajoz when, in the mayhem following the successful attack, a fine Spanish lady and her young sister threw themselves upon his protection, their ears bleeding from the wounds caused by British ruffians who had ripped out their earrings. Kincaid fell in love with the younger sister almost at once but was beaten to the punch by a fellow officer of the 95th. Although not named by Kincaid, the officer was, of course, Harry Smith and before too long he had married his young Spanish lady, Juana Maria de Los Dolores de Leon, who was to follow him faithfully throughout the rest of the war. When Smith was later knighted she became the very Lady Smith after whom the town in

South Africa was later named, the town which played host to a very different siege during the Boer War some 88 years after Badajoz. History would have been somewhat different if John Kincaid had moved a little quicker.

Kincaid's last campaign was Waterloo in 1815. With his comrades of the 95th he spent most of the momentous day in action in and about the sandpit which lay close to the farm of La Haye Sainte. Once again our hero came through unscathed to recount his experiences and our knowledge of the battle is all the richer for them. Kincaid also made a telling comment about the relative merits of the army in the Peninsula and that at Waterloo when he wrote, 'If Lord Wellington had been at the head of his old Peninsula army, I am confident that he would have swept his opponents off the face of the earth immediately after their first attack; but with such a heterogeneous mixture under his command, he was obliged to submit to a longer day.' The question of how Wellington would have fared with his old Peninsular army will, sadly, have to remain one of British military history's great 'what ifs', although I suspect Kincaid was not far from the truth.

Kincaid served with the 95th for a further sixteen years, being promoted Captain in 1826. He was knighted in 1852 after having been appointed Exon of the Royal Bodyguard of the Yeoman of the Guard in 1844. He died on April 22nd 1862. *Adventures in the Rifle Brigade* and *Random Shots from a Rifleman* represent history at its very best; informative, enlightening and perceptive, hard fact mixed with humour, a vivid portrayal of life on campaign in one of the most famous regiments in the British army, and most importantly, enjoyable and vastly entertaining.

Ian Fletcher
Rochester, 1998

ADVENTURES

IN THE

RIFLE BRIGADE,

IN THE

PENINSULA,

FRANCE, AND THE NETHERLANDS,

FROM 1809 TO 1815.

BY CAPTAIN J. KINCAID.

LONDON:

T. AND W. BOONE, STRAND.

M DCCCXXX.

CONTENTS.

CHAPTER I.

CHAP. II.

CHAP. III.

CHAP V.

CHAP. VI.

CHAP. IX.

CHAP. X.

CHAP. XI.

CHAP. XII.

CHAP. XIII.

CHAP. XIV.

CHAP. XV.

CHAP. XVI.

CHAP. XVII.

CHAP. XVIII.

CHAP. XIX.

CHAP. XX.

CHAP. XXI.

TO

MAJOR-GEN. SIR ANDREW BARNARD,

K. C. B.

COLONEL OF THE FIRST BATTALION RIFLE BRIGADE,

AND ITS LEADER

DURING A LONG AND BRILLIANT PERIOD

OF ITS HISTORY,

THIS VOLUME IS RESPECTFULLY INSCRIBED

BY HIS VERY OBEDIENT

AND VERY OBLIGED HUMBLE SERVANT,

J. KINCAID.

ADVERTISEMENT

In tracing the following scenes, I have chiefly drawn on the reminiscences of my military life, and endeavoured faithfully to convey to the mind of the reader the impression which they made on my own at the time of their occurrence. Should any errors, as to dates or trifling circumstances, have inadvertently crept into my narrative, I hope they will be ascribed to want of memory, rather than to any wilful intention to mislead. I am aware, that some objections may be taken to my style; for

> " Rude am I in my speech,
> And little bless'd with the set phrase of peace :
> For, since these arms of mine had seven years' pith,
> Till now, some nine moons wasted, they have us'd
> Their dearest action in the tented field :
> And little of this world can I speak,
> More than pertains to feats of broil and battle ;
> And therefore little shall I grace my cause
> In speaking for myself ; yet, by your gracious patience,
> I will a round unvarnished tale deliver,"

ADVENTURES

IN THE

RIFLE BRIGADE.

CHAPTER I.

Joined the Rifles. Walcheren Expedition. A young Soldier. A Marine View. Campaign in South Beeveland. Retreat to Scotland.

I JOINED the second battalion rifle brigade, (then the ninety-fifth,) at Hythe-Barracks, in the spring of 1809, and, in a month after, we proceeded to form a part of the expedition to Holland, under the Earl of Chatham.

With the usual Quixotic feelings of a youngster, I remember how very desirous I was, on

B

the march to Deal, to impress the minds of the
natives with a suitable notion of the magnitude
of my importance, by carrying a donkey-load
of pistols in my belt, and screwing my naturally
placid countenance up to a pitch of ferocity
beyond what it was calculated to bear.

We embarked in the Downs, on board the
Hussar frigate, and afterwards removed to the
Namur, a seventy-four, in which we were con-
veyed to our destination.

I had never before been in a ship of war, and
it appeared to me, the first night, as if the sailors
and marines did not pull well together, excepting
by the ears; for my hammock was slung over
the descent into the cockpit, and I had scarcely
turned-in when an officer of marines came and
abused his sentry for not seeing the lights out
below, according to orders. The sentry proceeded to explain, that the *middies* would not
put them out for him, when the naked shoulders
and the head of one of them, illuminated with
a red nightcap, made its appearance above the
hatchway, and began to take a lively share in

the argument. The marine officer, looking down, with some astonishment, demanded, " d—n you, sir, who are you ?" to which the head and shoulders immediately rejoined, " and d—n and b—t you, sir, who are you ?"

We landed on the island of South Beeveland, where we remained about three weeks, playing at soldiers, smoking *mynheer's* long clay pipes, and drinking his *vrow's* butter-milk, for which I paid liberally with my precious blood to their infernal musquittos ; not to mention that I had all the extra valour shaken out of me by a horrible ague, which commenced a campaign on my carcass, and compelled me to retire upon Scotland, for the aid of my native air, by virtue of which it was ultimately routed.

I shall not carry my first chapter beyond my first campaign, as I am anxious that my reader should not expend more than his first breath upon an event which cost too many their last.

CHAP. II.

Rejoin the Regiment. Embark for the Peninsula. Arrival
in the Tagus. The City of Lisbon, with its Contents.
Sail for Figuera. Landing extraordinary. Billet ditto.
The City of Coimbra. A hard Case. A cold Case, in
which a favourite Scotch Dance is introduced. Climate.
The Duke of Wellington.

I REJOINED the battalion, at Hythe, in the
spring of 1810, and, finding that the company
to which I belonged had embarked, to join the
first battalion in the Peninsula, and that they
were waiting at Spithead for a fair wind, I immediately applied, and obtained permission, to join
them.

We were about the usual time at sea, and
indulged in the usual amusements, beginning
with keeping journals, in which I succeeded in

inserting two remarks on the state of the weather, when I found my inclination for book-making superseded by the more disagreeable study of appearing eminently happy under an irresistible inclination towards sea-sickness. We anchored in the Tagus in September;—no thanks to the ship, for she was a leaky one, and wishing foul winds to the skipper, for he was a bad one.

To look at Lisbon from the Tagus, there are few cities in the universe that can promise so much, and none, I hope, that can keep it so badly.

I only got on shore one day, for a few hours, and, as I never again had an opportunity of correcting the impression, I have no objection to its being considered an uncharitable one; but I wandered for a time amid the abominations of its streets and squares, in the vain hope that I had got involved among a congregation of stables and outhouses; but when I was, at length, compelled to admit it as the miserable apology for the fair city that I had seen from the harbour, I began to contemplate, with astonishment, and no little amusement, the very appropriate appearance of its inhabitants.

The church, I concluded, had, on that occasion, indulged her numerous offspring with a holiday, for they occupied a much larger portion of the streets than all the world besides. Some of them were languidly strolling about, and looking the sworn foes of time, while others crowded the doors of the different coffee-houses; the fat jolly-looking friars cooling themselves with lemonade, and the lean mustard-pot-faced ones sipping coffee out of thimble-sized cups, with as much caution as if it had been physic.

The next class that attracted my attention was the numerous collection of well-starved dogs, who were indulging in all the luxury of extreme poverty on the endless dung-heaps.

There, too, sat the industrious citizen, basking in the sunshine of his shop-door, and gathering in the flock which is so bountifully reared on his withered tribe of children. There strutted the spruce cavalier, with his upper-man furnished at the expense of his lower, and looking ridiculously imposing: and there—but sacred be their daughters, for the sake of *one*, who shed a lustre over her squalid sisterhood, sufficiently brilliant to redeem their whole nation from the odious sin of ugliness. I was looking for an official person, living somewhere near the Convent D'Estrella, and was endeavouring to express my wishes to a boy, when I heard a female voice, in broken English, from a balcony above, giving the information I desired. I looked up, and saw a young girl, dressed in white, who was loveliness itself! In the few words which passed between us, of lively unconstrained civility on her part, and pure confounded gratitude on mine, she seemed so perfectly after my own heart, that she lit a torch in it which burnt for two years and a half.

It must not detract from her merits that she was almost the only one that I saw during that period in which it was my fate to tread war's roughest, rudest path,—daily staring his grim majesty out of countenance, and nightly slumbering on the cold earth, or in the tenantless mansion, for I felt as if she would have been the chosen companion of my waking dreams in *rosier* walks, as I never recalled the fair vision to my aid, even in the worst of times, that it did not act upon my drooping spirits like a glass of brandy.

It pleased the great disposer of naval events to remove us to another and a better ship, and to send us off for Figuera, next day, with a foul wind.

Sailing at the rate of one mile in two hours, we reached Figuera's Bay at the end of eight days, and were welcomed by about a hundred hideous looking Portuguese women, whose joy was so excessive that they waded up to their arm-pits through a heavy surf, and insisted on carrying us on shore on their backs! I never clearly ascertained whether they had been ac-tuated by the purity of love or gold.

Our men were lodged for the night in a large barn, and the officers billetted in town. Mine chanced to be on the house of a mad-woman, whose extraordinary appearance I never shall forget. Her petticoats scarcely reached to the knee, and all above the lower part of the bosom was bare; and though she looked not more than middle aged, her skin seemed as if it had been regularly prepared to receive the impression of her last will and testament; her head was defended by a chevaux-de-frise of black wiry hair, which pointed fiercely in every direction, while her eyes looked like two burnt holes in a blanket. I had no sooner opened the door than she stuck her arms a-kimbo, and, opening a mouth, which stretched from ear to ear, she began vociferating " *bravo, bravissimo !*"

Being a stranger alike to the appearance and the manners of the natives, I thought it possible that the former might have been nothing out of the common run, and concluding that she was overjoyed at seeing her country reenforced, at that perilous moment, by a fellow upwards of six feet high, and thinking it necessary to sympathize in some degree in her patriotic feelings, I began to " *bravo*" too ; but as her second shout ascended ten degrees, and kept increasing in that ratio, until it amounted to absolute frenzy, I faced to the right-about, and, before our *tête-à-tête* had lasted the brief space of three-quarters of a minute, I disappeared with all possible haste, her terrific yells vibrating in my astonished ears long after I had turned the corner of the street; nor did I feel perfectly at ease until I found myself stretched on a bundle of straw in a corner of the barn occupied by the men.

We proceeded, next morning, to join the army; and, as our route lay through the city of Coimbra, we came to the magnanimous resolution of providing ourselves with all manner of comforts and equipments for the campaign on our arrival there; but, when we entered it, at the end of the second day, our disappointment was quite eclipsed by astonishment at finding ourselves the only living things in a city, which ought to have been furnished with twenty thousand souls.

Lord Wellington was then in the course of his retreat from the frontiers of Spain to the lines of Torres Vedras, and had compelled the inhabitants on the line of march to abandon their homes, and to destroy or carry away every thing that could be of service to the enemy. It was a measure that ultimately saved their country, though ruinous and distressing to those concerned, and on no class of individuals did it bear harder, for the moment, than our own little detachment, a company of rosy-cheeked, chubbed youths, who, after three months feeding on ship's dumplings, were thus thrust, at a moment of extreme activity, in the face of an advancing foe, supported by a pound of raw beef, drawn every day fresh from the bullock, and a mouldy biscuit.

The difficulties we encountered were nothing out of the usual course of old campaigners; but, untrained and unprovided as I was, I still looked back upon the twelve or fourteen days following the battle of Busaco as the most trying I have ever experienced, for we were on our legs from day-light until dark, in daily contact with the enemy; and, to satisfy the stomach of an ostrich, I had, as already stated, only a pound of beef, a pound of biscuit, and one glass of rum. A brother-officer was kind enough to strap my boat-cloak and portmanteau on the mule carrying his heavy baggage, which, on account of the proximity of the foe, was never permitted to be within a day's march of us, so that, in addition to my simple uniform, my only covering every night was the canopy of heaven, from whence the dews descended so refreshingly, that I generally awoke, at the end of an hour, chilled, and wet to the skin; and I could only purchase an equal length of additional repose by jumping up and running about, until I acquired a sleeping quantity of warmth. Nothing in life can be more ridiculous than seeing a lean, lank fellow start from a profound sleep, at midnight, and begin lashing away at the highland fling, as if St. Andrew himself had been playing the bagpipes; but it was a measure that I very often had recourse to, as the cleverest method of producing heat. In short, though the prudent general may preach the propriety of light baggage in the enemy's presence, I will ever maintain that there is marvellous small personal comfort in travelling so fast and so lightly as I did.

The Portuguese farmers will tell you that the beauty of their climate consists in their crops receiving from the nightly dews the refreshing influence of a summer's shower, and that they ripen in the daily sun. But *they* are a sordid set of rascals! Whereas *I* speak with the enlightened views of a man of war, and say, that it is poor consolation to me, after having been deprived of my needful repose, and kept all night in a fever, dancing wet and cold, to be told that I shall be warm enough in the morning? it is like frying a person after he has been boiled; and I insisted upon it, that if their sun had been milder and their dews lighter that I should have found it much more pleasant.

THE DUKE OF WELLINGTON.

From the moment that I joined the army, so intense was my desire to get a look at this illustrious chief, that I never should have forgiven the Frenchman that had killed me before I effected it. My curiosity did not remain long ungratified; for, as our post was next the enemy, I found, when any thing was to be done, that it was his also. He was just such a man as I had figured in my mind's eye, and I thought that the stranger would betray a grievous want of penetration who could not select the Duke of Wellington from amid five hundred in the same uniform.

CHAP. III.

Other People, Myself, and my Regiment. Retreat to the Lines of Torres Vedras. Leave Coimbra, followed by a select group of Natives. Ford the Streets of Condacia in good spirits. A Provost-Marshal and his favourites. A fall. Convent of Batalha. Turned out of Allenquer. Passed through Sobral. Turned into Arruda. Quartering of the Light Division, and their Quarters at Arruda. Burial of an only Child. Lines of Torres Vedras. Difference of opinion between Massena and Myself. Military Customs.

HAVING now brought myself regularly into the field, under the renowned Wellington, should this narrative, by any accident, fall into the hands of others who served there, and who may be unreasonable enough to expect their names to be mentioned in it, let me tell them that

they are most confoundedly mistaken! Every
man may write a book for himself, if he likes,
but *this* is mine; and, as I borrow no man's
story, neither will I give any man a particle of
credit for his deeds, as I have got so little for
my own that I have none to spare. Neither
will I mention any regiment but my own, if I
can possibly avoid it, for there is none other that
I like so much, and none else so much deserves
it; for we were the light regiment of the Light
Division, and fired the first and last shot in
almost every battle, siege, and skirmish, in
which the army was engaged during the war.

In stating the foregoing resolution, however,
with regard to regiments, I beg to be understood
as identifying our old and gallant associates, the
forty-third and fifty-second, as a part of ourselves, for they bore their share in every thing,
and I love them as I hope to do my better half,
(when I come to be divided,) wherever *we* were,
they were ; and although the nature of our arm
generally gave us more employment in the way
of skirmishing, yet, whenever it came to a pinch,

independent of a suitable mixture of them among
us, we had only to look behind to see a line, in
which we might place a degree of confidence,
almost equal to our hopes in heaven; nor were
we ever disappointed. There never was a corps
of riflemen in the hands of such supporters!

October 1st, 1810.—We stood to our arms at
day light this morning, on a hill in front of
Coimbra; and, as the enemy soon after came
on in force, we retired before them through the
city. The civil authorities, in making their own
hurried escape, had totally forgotten that they
had left a gaol full of rogues unprovided for,
and who, as we were passing near them, made
the most hideous screaming for relief. Our
quarter-master-general very humanely took some
men, who broke open the doors, and the whole
of them were soon seen howling along the bridge
into the wide world, in the most delightful delirium, with the French dragoons at their
heels.

We retired, the same night, through Condacia,
where the commissariat were destroying quanti-

ties of stores that they were unable to carry off. They handed out shoes and shirts to any one that would take them, and the streets were literally running ankle deep with rum, in which the soldiers were dipping their cups and helping themselves as they marched along. The commissariat, some years afterwards, called for a return of the men who had received shirts and shoes on this occasion, with a view of making us pay for them, but we very briefly replied that the one half were dead, and the other half would be d——d before they would pay any thing.

We retired this day to Leria, and, at the entrance of the city, saw an English and a Portuguese soldier dangling by the bough of a tree— the first summary example I had ever seen of martial law.

A provost-marshal, on actual service, is a character of considerable pretensions, as he can flog at pleasure, always moves about with a guard of honour, and though he cannot altogether stop a man's breath without an order, yet, when he is ordered to hang a given number out of a crowd of plunderers, his *friends* are not particularly designated, so that he can invite any one that he takes a fancy to, to follow him to the nearest tree, where he, without further ceremony, relieves him from the cares and troubles of this wicked world.

There was only one *furnished* shop remaining in the town at this time, and I went in to see what they had got to sell; but I had scarcely past the threshold when I heard a tremendous clatter at my heels, as if the opposite house had been pitched in at the door after me; and, on wheeling round to ascertain the cause, I found, when the dust cleared away, that a huge stone balcony, with iron railings, which had been over the door, overcharged with a collection of old wives looking at the troops, had tumbled down; and in spite of their vociferations for the aid of their patron saints, some them were considerably damaged.

We halted one night near the convent of Batalha, one of the finest buildings in Portugal.

It has, I believe, been clearly established, that a living man in ever so bad health is better than two dead ones; but it appears that the latter will vary in value according to circumstances, for we found here, in very high preservation, the body of King John of Portugal, who founded the edifice in commemoration of some victory, God knows how long ago; and though he would have been reckoned a highly valuable antique, within a glass case, in an apothecary's hall in England, yet he was held so cheap in his own house, that the very finger which most probably pointed the way to the victory alluded to, is now in the baggage of the Rifle Brigade! Reader, point not *thy* finger at me, for I am not the man.

Retired on the morning of a very wet, stormy day to Allenquer, a small town on the top of a mountain, surrounded by still higher ones; and, as the enemy had not shewn themselves the evening before, we took possession of the houses, with a tolerable prospect of being permitted the unusual treat of eating a dinner under cover.

But by the time that the pound of beef was parboiled, and while an officer of dragoons was in the act of reporting that he had just patrolled six leagues to the front, without seeing any signs of an enemy, we saw the indefatigable rascals, on the mountain opposite our windows, just beginning to wind round us, with a mixture of cavalry and infantry; the wind blowing so strong, that the long tail of each particular horse stuck as stiffly out in the face of the one behind, as if the whole had been strung upon a cable and dragged by the leaders. We turned out a few companies, and kept them in check while the division was getting under arms, spilt the soup as usual, and transferring the smoking solids to the haversack, for future mastication, we continued our retreat.

We past through the town of Sobral, soon after dark, the same night; and, by the aid of some rushlights in a window, saw two apothecaries, the very counterparts of Romeo's, who were the only remnants of the place, and had braved the horrors of war for the sake of the gallipots, and in the hopes that their profession would be held sacred. They were both on the same side of the counter, looking each other point blank in the face, their sharp noses not three inches apart, and neither daring to utter a syllable, but both listening intensely to the noise outside. Whatever their courage might have been screwed up to before, it was evident that we were indebted for their presence now to their fears; and their appearance altogether was so ludicrous, that they excited universal shouts of laughter as they came within view of the successive divisions.

Our long retreat ended at midnight, on our arrival at the handsome little town of Arruda, which was destined to be the piquet post of our division, in front of the fortified lines. The quartering of our division, whether by night or by day, was an affair of about five minutes. The quarter-master-general preceded the troops, accompanied by the brigade-majors and the quarter-masters of regiments; and after marking off certain houses for his general and staff, he split the remainder of the town between the majors of brigades: they in their turn provided for their generals and staff, and then made a wholesale division of streets among the quartermasters of regiments, who, after providing for their commanding officers and staff, retailed the remaining houses, in equal proportions, among the companies; so that, by the time that the regiment arrived, there was nothing to be done beyond the quarter-master's simply telling each captain, " here's a certain number of houses for you."

Like all other places on the line of march, we found Arruda totally deserted, and its inhabitants had fled in such a hurry, that the keys of their house doors were the only things they carried away; so that when we got admission, through our usual key,* we were not a little gratified to find that the houses were not only regularly furnished, but most of them had some food in the larder, and a plentiful supply of

* Transmitting a rifle-ball through the key-hole: it opens every lock.

good wines in the cellar; and, in short, that
they only required a few lodgers capable of
appreciating the good things which the gods
had provided; and the deuce is in it if we were
not the very folks who could !

Unfortunately for ourselves, and still more so
for the proprietors, we never dreamt of the
possibility of our being able to keep possession
of the town, as we thought it a matter of course
that the enemy would attack our lines; and, as
this was only an outpost, that it must fall into
their hands; so that, in conformity with the
system upon which we had all along been retreating, we destroyed every thing that we could
not use ourselves, to prevent their benefiting by
it. But, when we continued to hold the post
beyond the expected period, our indiscretion was
visited on our own heads, as we had destroyed
in a day what would have made us luxurious
for months. We were in hopes that, afterwards,
the enemy would have forced the post, if only
for an hour, that we might have saddled them
with the mischief; but, as they never even made

the attempt, it left it in the power of ill-natured people to say, that we had plundered one of our own towns. This was the only instance during the war in which the light division had reason to blush for their conduct, and even in that we had the law martial on our side, whatever gospel law might have said against it.

The day after our arrival, Mr. Simmons and myself had the curiosity to look into the church, which was in nowise injured, and was fitted up in a style of magnificence becoming such a town. The body of a poor old woman was there, lying dead before the altar. It seemed as if she had been too infirm to join in the general flight, and had just dragged herself to that spot by a last effort of nature, and expired. We immediately determined, that as hers was the only body that we had found in the town, either alive or dead, that she should have more glory in the grave than she appeared to have enjoyed on this side of it; and, with our united exertions, we succeeded in raising a marble slab, which surmounted a monumental vault, and was beauti-

c

fully embellished with armorial blazonry, and, depositing the body inside, we replaced it again carefully. If the personage to whom it belonged happened to have a tenant of his own for it soon afterwards, he must have been rather astonished at the manner in which the apartment was occupied.

Those who wish a description of the lines of Torres Vedras, must read *Napier*, or some one else who knows all about them; for my part, I know nothing, excepting that I was told that one end of them rested on the Tagus, and the other somewhere on the sea; and I saw, with my own eyes, a variety of redoubts and field-works on the various hills which stand between. This, however, I do know, that we have since kicked the French out of more formidable looking and stronger places; and, with all due deference be it spoken, I think that the Prince of Essling ought to have tried his luck against them, as he could only have been beaten by fighting, as he afterwards was without it! And if he thinks that he would have lost as many men by trying, as he did by not trying, he must allow me to differ in opinion with him.

In very warm or very wet weather it was customary to put us under cover in the town during the day, but we were always moved back to our bivouac, on the heights, during the night; and it was rather amusing to observe the different notions of individual comfort, in the selection of furniture, which officers transferred from their *town house* to their *no house* on the heights. A sofa, or a mattress, one would have thought most likely to be put in requisition; but it was not unusual to see a full-length looking-glass preferred to either.

The post of the company to which I belonged, on the heights, was near a redoubt, immediately behind Arruda; there was a cattle-shed near it, which we cleaned out, and used as a sort of quarter. On turning out from breakfast one morning, we found that the butcher had been about to offer up the usual sacrifice of a bullock to the wants of the day;

but it had broken loose, and, in trying to regain his victim, had caught it by the tail, which he twisted round his hand; and, when we made our appearance, they were performing a variety of evolutions at a gallop, to the great amusement of the soldiers; until an unlucky turn brought them down upon our house, which had been excavated out of the face of the hill, on which the upper part of the roof rested, and *in* they went, heels over head, butcher, bullock, tail and all, bearing down the whole fabric with a tremendous crash.

N. B. It was very fortunate that we happened to be outside; and very unfortunate, as we were now obliged to remain out.

We certainly lived in *clover* while we remained here; every thing we saw was our own, seeing no one there who had a more legitimate claim; and every field was a vineyard. Ultimately it was considered too much trouble to pluck the grapes, as there were a number of poor native thieves in the habit of coming from the rear, every day, to steal some, so that a soldier had nothing to do but to watch one until he was marching off with his basket full, when he would very deliberately place his back against that of the Portuguese, and relieve him of his load, without wasting any words about the bargain. The poor wretch would follow the soldier to the camp, in the hope of having his basket returned, as it generally was, when emptied.

Massena conceiving any attack upon our lines to be hopeless, as his troops were rapidly mouldering away with sickness and want, at length began to withdraw them nearer to the source of his supplies.

He abandoned his position, opposite to us, on the night of the 9th of November, leaving some stuffed-straw gentlemen occupying their usual posts. Some of them were cavalry, some infantry, and they seemed such respectable representatives of their spectral predecessors, that, in the haze of the following morning, we thought that they had been joined by some well-fed ones from the rear; and it was late in the day before we discovered the mistake and advanced in pursuit. In passing by the edge of a mill-pond, after dark, our adjutant and his horse tumbled in, and, as the latter had no tail to hold on by, they were both very nearly drowned.

It was late ere we halted for the night, on the side of the road, near to Allenquer, and I got under cover in a small house, which looked as if it had been honoured as the head-quarters of the tailor-general of the French army, for the floor was strewed with variegated threads, various complexioned buttons, with particles and remnants of *cabbage;* and, if it could not boast of the flesh and fowl of Noah's ark, there was an abundance of the creeping things which it were to be wished that that commander had not left behind. We marched before day-light next morning, leaving a *rousing* fire in the chimney, which shortly became too small to hold it; for we had not proceeded far before we perceived that the well-dried thatched roof had joined in the general blaze, a circumstance which caused us no little uneasiness, for our general, the late

Major-general Robert Crawford, had brought us up in the fear of our master; and, as he was a sort of person who would not see a fire, of that kind, in the same *light* that we did, I was by no means satisfied that my commission lay snug in my pocket, until we had fairly marched it out of sight, and in which we were aided not a little by a slight fire of another kind, which he was required to watch with the advanced guard.

On our arrival at Vallé, on the 12th of Nov. we found the enemy behind the Rio Maior, occupying the heights of Santarem, and exchanged some shots with their advanced posts. In the course of the night we experienced one of those tremendous thunder-storms which used to precede the Wellington victories, and which induced us to expect a general action on the following day. I had disposed myself to sleep in a beautiful green hollow way, and, before I had time even to dream of the effects of their heavy rains, I found myself floating most majestically towards the river, in a fair way of becoming

food for the fishes. I ever after gave those in-
viting-looking spots a wide birth, as I found
that they were regular watercourses.

Next morning our division crossed the river,
and commenced a false attack on the enemy's
left, with a view of making them show their
force; and it was to have been turned into a
real attack, if their position was found to be
occupied by a rear guard only; but, after keeping up a smart skirmishing-fire the greater part
of the day, Lord Wellington was satisfied that
their whole army was present, we were consequently withdrawn.

This affair terminated the campaign of 1810.
Our division took possession of the village of
Vallé and its adjacents, and the rest of the army
was placed in cantonments, under whatever cover
the neighbouring country afforded.

Our battalion was stationed in some empty
farm-houses, near the end of the bridge of Santarem, which was nearly half a mile long; and
our sentries and those of the enemy were within
pistol-shot of each other on the bridge.

I do not mean to insinuate that a country is never so much at peace as when at open war, but I do say that a soldier can no where sleep so soundly, nor is he any where so secure from surprise, as when within musket-shot of his enemy.

We lay four months in this situation, divided only by a rivulet, without once exchanging shots. Every evening, at the hour

" When bucks to dinner go,
And cits to sup,"

it was our practice to dress for sleep: we saddled our horses, buckled on our armour, and lay down, with the bare floor for a bed and a stone for a pillow, ready for any thing, and reckless of every thing but the honour of our corps and country; for I will say (to save the expense of a trumpeter) that a more devoted set of fellows were never associated.

We stood to our arms every morning at an hour before daybreak, and remained there until a *grey horse* could be seen a mile off, (which is the military criterion by which daylight is acknowledged, and the hour of surprise past,) when we proceeded to unharness, and to indulge in such *luxuries* as our toilet and our table afforded.

The Maior, as far as the bridge of Vallé, was navigable for the small craft from Lisbon, so that our table, while we remained there, cut as respectable a figure, as regular supplies of rice, salt fish, and potatoes could make it; not to mention that our pigskin was, at all times, at least three parts full of a common red wine, which used to be dignified by the name of *blackstrap*. We had the utmost difficulty, however, in keeping up appearances in the way of dress. The jacket, in spite of shreds and patches, always maintained something of the original about it; but woe befel the regimental smallclothes, and they could only be replaced by very extraordinary apologies, of which I remember that I had two pair at this period, *one* of a common brown Portuguese cloth, and the *other,* or Sunday's pair, of black velvet. We had no women with the regiment; and the ceremony of washing a shirt amounted to my servant's taking it by the collar, and giving it a couple of shakes in the water, and then hanging it up to dry. Smoothing-irons were not the fashion of the times, and, if a fresh well-dressed aide-de-camp did occasionally come from England, we used to stare at him with about as much respect as Hotspur did at his " waiting gentlewoman."

The winter here was uncommonly mild. I am not the sort of person to put myself much in the way of ice, except on a warm summer's day; but the only inconvenience that I felt in bathing, in the middle of December, was the quantity of leeches that used to attach themselves to my personal supporters, obliging me to cut a few capers to shake them off, after leaving the water.

Our piquet-post, at the bridge, became a regular lounge, for the winter, to all manner of folks.

I used to be much amused at seeing our naval officers come up from Lisbon riding on mules, with huge ships' spy-glasses, like six-pounders, strapped across the backs of their saddles. Their first question invariably was, " Who is that fellow there," (pointing to the enemy's sentry, close to us,) and, on being told that he was a Frenchman, " Then why the devil don't you shoot him!"

Repeated acts of civility passed between the French and us during this tacit suspension of hostilities. The greyhounds of an officer followed a hare, on one occasion, into their lines, and they very politely returned them.

I was one night on piquet, at the end of the bridge, when a ball came from the French sentry and struck the burning billet of wood round which we were sitting, and they sent in a flag of truce, next morning, to apologize for the accident, and to say that it had been done by a stupid fellow of a sentry, who imagined that people were advancing upon him. We admitted the apology, though we knew well enough that it had been done by a malicious rather than a stupid fellow, from the situation we occupied.

General Junot, one day reconnoitring, was severely wounded by a sentry, and Lord Wellington, knowing that they were at that time destitute of every thing in the shape of comfort, sent to request his acceptance of any thing that Lisbon afforded that could be of any service to him; but the French general was too much of a politician to admit the want of any thing.

CHAP. V.

Campaign of 1811 opens. Massena's Retreat. Wretched Condition of the Inhabitants on the Line of March. Affairs with the Enemy, near Pombal. Description of a Bivouac. Action near Redinha. Destruction of Condacia and Action near it. Burning of the Village of Illama, and Misery of its Inhabitants. Action at Foz D'Aronce. Confidential Servants with Donkey-Assistants.

THE campaign of 1811 commenced on the 6th of March, by the retreat of the enemy from Santarem.

Lord Wellington seemed to be perfectly acquainted with their intentions, for he sent to apprize our piquets, the evening before, that they were going off, and to desire that they should feel for them occasionally during the night, and give the earliest information of their having started. It was not, however, until day-light that we were quite certain of their having gone, and our division was instantly put in motion after them, passing through the town of Santarem, around which their camp fires were still burning.

Santarem is finely situated, and probably had been a handsome town. I had never seen it in prosperity, and it now looked like a city of the plague, represented by empty dogs and empty houses; and, but for the tolling of a con-vent-bell by some unseen hand, its appearance was altogether inhuman.

We halted for the night near Pyrnes. This little town, and the few wretched inhabitants who had been induced to remain in it under the faith-less promises of the French generals, shewed fearful signs of a late visit from a barbarous and merciless foe. Young women were lying in their houses brutally violated,—the streets were strewed with broken furniture, intermixed with the putrid carcasses of murdered peasants, mules, and donkeys, and every description of filth, that filled the air with pestilential nausea. The few starved male inhabitants who were stalking amid the wreck of their friends and property, looked like so many skeletons who had been permitted to leave their graves for the purpose of taking vengeance on their oppressors, and the mangled body of every Frenchman who was unfortunate or imprudent enough to stray from his column, shewed how religiously they performed their mission.

March 8th.—We overtook their rear guard this evening, snugly put up for the night in a little village, the name of which I do not recollect, but a couple of six pounders, supported by a few of our rifles, induced them to extend their walk.

March 9th.—While moving along the road this morning, we found a man, who had deserted from us a short time before, in the uniform of a French dragoon, with his head laid open by one of our bullets. He was still alive, exciting any thing but sympathy among his former associates. Towards the afternoon we found the enemy in force, on the plain in front of Pombal, where we exchanged some shots.

March 11th.—They retired yesterday to the heights behind Pombal, with their advanced posts occupying the town and moorish castle, which our battalion, assisted by some Cácadores, attacked this morning, and drove them from with considerable loss. Dispositions were then made for a general attack on their position, but the other divisions of our army did not arrive until too late in the evening. We bivouacked for the night in a ploughed field, under the castle, with our sentries within pistol shot, while it rained in torrents.

As it is possible that some of my readers might never have had the misfortune to experience the comforts of a bivouac, and as the one which I am now in, contains but a small quantity of sleep, I shall devote a waking hour for their edification.

When a regiment arrives at its ground for the night, it is formed in columns of companies, at full, half, or quarter distance, according to the space which circumstances will permit it to occupy.   The officer commanding each company then receives his orders; and, after communicating whatever may be necessary to the men, he desires them to " pile arms, and make themselves comfortable for the night."   Now, I pray thee, most sanguine reader, suffer not thy fervid imagination to transport thee into elysian fields at the pleasing exhortation conveyed in the concluding part of the captain's address, but rest thee contentedly in the one where it is made, which in all probability is a ploughed one, and that, too, in a state of preparation to take a model of thy very beautiful person, under the melting influence of a shower of rain.   The soldiers of each company have a hereditary claim to the ground next to their arms, as have their officers to a wider range on the same line, limited to the end of a bugle sound, if not by a neighbouring corps, or one that is not neighbourly, for the nearer a man is to his enemy, the nearer he likes to be to his friends.   Suffice it, that each individual knows his place as well as if he had been born on the estate, and takes immediate possession accordingly. In a ploughed or a stubble field there is scarcely a choice of quarters; but, whenever there is a sprinkling of trees, it is always an object to secure a good one, as it affords shelter from the sun by day and the dews by night, besides being a sort of home or sign post for a group of officers, as denoting the best place of entertainment; for they hang their spare clothing and accoutrements among the branches, barricade themselves on each side with their saddles, canteens, and portmanteaus, and, with a blazing fire in their front, they indulge, according to their various humours, in a complete state of gipsyfication.

There are several degrees of comfort to be reckoned in a bivouac, two of which will suffice.

The first, and worst, is to arrive at the end of a cold wet day, too dark to see your ground, and too near the enemy to be permitted to unpack the knapsacks or to take off accoutre-

ments; where, unincumbered with baggage or
eatables of any kind, you have the consolation of
knowing that things are now at their worst, and
that any change must be for the better. You
keep yourself alive for a while, in collecting
material to feed your fire with. You take a smell
at your empty calibash, which recalls to your
remembrance the delicious flavour of its last
drop of wine. You curse your servant for not
having contrived to send you something or other
from the baggage, (though you know that it was
impossible). You then damn the enemy for
being so near you, though probably, as in the
present instance, it was you that came so near
them. And, finally, you take a whiff at the
end of a cigar, if you have one, and keep
grumbling through the smoke, like distant thunder through a cloud, until you tumble into a
most warlike sleep.

The next, and most common one, is, when you
are not required to look quite so sharp, and when
the light baggage and provisions come in at the
heel of the regiment. If it is early in the day,

the first thing to be done is to make some tea, the most sovereign restorative for jaded spirits. We then proceed to our various duties. The officers of each company form a mess of themselves. One remains in camp to attend to the duties of the regiment; a second attends to the mess; he goes to the regimental butcher, and bespeaks a portion of the only purchaseable commodities, hearts, livers, and kidneys; and also to see whether he cannot *do* the commissary out of a few extra biscuit, or a canteen of brandy; and the remainder are gentlemen at large for the day. But while they go hunting among the neighbouring regiments for news, and the neighbouring houses for curiosity, they have always an eye to their mess, and omit no opportunity of adding to the general stock.

Dinner hour, for fear of accidents, is always the hour when dinner can be got ready; and the 14th section of the articles of war is always most rigidly attended to, by every good officer parading himself round the camp-kettle at the time fixed, with his haversack in his hand. A

haversack on service is a sort of dumb waiter.
The mess have a good many things in common,
but the contents of the haversack are exclusively
the property of its owner ; and a well regulated
one ought never to be without the following-
furniture, unless when the perishable part is
consumed, in consequence of every other means
of supply having failed, viz. a couple of biscuit,
a sausage, a little tea and sugar, a knife, fork,
and spoon, a tin cup, (which answers to the
names of *tea-cup, soup-plate, wine-glass,* and
tumbler,) a pair of socks, a piece of soap, a
tooth-brush, towel, and comb, and half a dozen
cigars.

After doing justice to the dinner, if we feel in
a humour for additional society, we transfer ourselves to some neighbouring mess, taking our
cups, and whatever we mean to drink, along
with us, for in those times there is nothing to
be expected from our friends beyond the pleasure of their conversation : and, finally, we retire
to rest. To avoid inconvenience by the tossing
off of the bed-clothes, each officer has a blanket

sewed up at the sides, like a sack, into which he scrambles, and, with a green sod or a smooth stone for a pillow, composes himself to sleep; and, under such a glorious reflecting canopy as the heavens, it would be a subject of mortification to an astronomer to see the celerity with which he tumbles into it. Habit gives endurance, and fatigue is the best night-cap; no matter that the veteran's countenance is alternately stormed with torrents of rain, heavy dews, and hoar-frosts; no matter that his ears are assailed by a million mouths of chattering locusts, and by some villanous donkey, who every half hour pitches a *bray* note, which, as a congregation of presbyterians follow their clerk, is instantly taken up by every mule and donkey in the army, and sent echoing from regiment to regiment, over hill and valley, until it dies away in the distance; no matter that the scorpion is lurking beneath his pillow, the snake winding his slimy way by his side, and the lizard galloping over his face, wiping his eyes with its long cold tail.

All are unheeded, until the warning voice of the brazen instrument sounds to arms. Strange it is, that the ear which is impervious to what would disturb the rest of the world besides, should alone be alive to one, and that, too, a sound which is likely to sooth the sleep of the citizens, or at most, to set them dreaming of their loves. But so it is: the first note of the melodious bugle places the soldier on his legs, like lightning; when, muttering a few curses at the unseasonableness of the hour, he plants himself on his alarm post, without knowing or caring about the cause.

Such is a bivouac; and our sleep-breaker having just sounded, the reader will find what occurred, by reading on.

March 12th.—We stood to our arms before day-light. Finding that the enemy had quitted the position in our front, we proceeded to follow them; and had not gone far before we heard the usual morning's salutation, of a couple of shots, between their rear and our advanced guard. On driving in their outposts, we found their whole army drawn out on the plain, near Redinha, and instantly quarrelled with them on a large scale.

As every body has read Waverley and the Scottish Chiefs, and knows that one battle is just like another, inasmuch as they always conclude by one or both sides running away; and as it is nothing to me what this or t'other regiment did, nor do I care three buttons what this or t'other person thinks he did, I shall limit all my descriptions to such events as immediately concerned the important personage most interested in this history.

Be it known then, that I was one of a crowd of skirmishers who were enabling the French ones to carry the news of their own defeat through a thick wood, at an infantry canter, when I found myself all at once within a few yards of one of their regiments in line, which opened such a fire, that had I not, rifleman like, taken instant advantage of the cover of a good fir tree, my name would have unquestionably been transmitted to posterity by that night's gazette. And,

D

however opposed it may be to the usual system of drill, I will maintain, from that day's experience, that the cleverest method of teaching a recruit to stand at attention, is to place him behind a tree and fire balls at him; as, had our late worthy disciplinarian, Sir David Dundas, himself, been looking on, I think that even *he* must have admitted that he never saw any one stand so fiercely upright as I did behind mine, while the balls were rapping into it as fast as if a fellow had been hammering a nail on the opposite side, not to mention the numbers that were whistling past, within the eighth of an inch of every part of my body, both before and behind, particularly in the vicinity of my nose, for which the upper part of the tree could barely afford protection.

This was a last and a desperate stand made by their rear-guard, for their own safety, immediately above the town, as their sole chance of escape depended upon their being able to hold the post until the only bridge across the river was clear of the other fugitives. But they could not hold it long enough; for, while we were undergoing a temporary sort of purgatory in their front, our comrades went working round their flanks, which quickly sent them flying, with us intermixed, at full cry, down the streets.

Whether in love or war, I have always considered that the pursuer has a decided advantage over the pursued. In the first, he may gain and cannot lose; but, in the latter, when one sees his enemy at full speed before him, one has such a peculiar conscious sort of feeling that he is on the right side, that I would not exchange places for any consideration.

When we reached the bridge, the scene became exceedingly interesting, for it was choked up by the fugitives who were, as usual, impeding each other's progress, and we did not find that the application of our swords to those nearest to us tended at all towards lessening their disorder, for it induced about a hundred of them to rush into an adjoining house for shelter, but that was getting regularly out of the frying-pan into the fire, for the house happened to be really in flames, and too hot to hold them, so that the same hundred were quickly seen unkennelling again, half-cooked, into the very jaws of their consumers.

John Bull, however, is not a blood-thirsty person, so that those who could not better themselves, had only to submit to a simple transfer of personal property to ensure his protection. We, consequently, made many prisoners at the bridge, and followed their army about a league beyond it, keeping up a flying fight until dark.

Just as Mr. Simmons and myself had crossed the river, and were talking over the events of the day, not a yard asunder, there was a Portuguese soldier in the act of passing between us, when a cannon-ball plunged into his belly—his head doubled down to his feet, and he stood for a moment in that posture before he rolled over a lifeless lump.

March 13th.—Arrived on the hill above Condacia in time to see that handsome little town in flames. Every species of barbarity continued to mark the enemy's retreating steps. They burnt every town or village through which they passed, and if we entered a church, which, by accident, had been spared, it was to see the murdered bodies of the peasantry on the altar.

While Lord Wellington, with his staff, was on a hill a little in front of us, waiting the result of a flank-movement which he had directed, some of the enemy's sharpshooters stole, unperceived, very near to him and began firing, but, fortunately, without effect. We immediately detached a few of ours to meet them, but the others ran off on their approach.

We lay by our arms until towards evening, when the enemy withdrew a short distance behind Condacia, and we closed up to them. There was a continued popping between the advanced posts all night.

March 14th.—Finding, at day-light, that the enemy still continued to hold the strong ground before us, some divisions of the army were sent to turn their flanks, while ours attacked them in front.

We drove them from one strong hold to

another, over a large track of very difficult country, mountainous and rocky, and thickly intersected with stone walls, and were involved in one continued hard skirmish from day-light until dark. This was the most harassing day's fighting that I ever experienced.

Day-light left the two armies looking at each other, near the village of Illama. The smoking roofs of the houses showed that the French had just quitted and, as usual, set fire to it, when the company to which I belonged was ordered on piquet there for the night. After posting our sentries, my brother-officer and myself had the curiosity to look into a house, and were shocked to find in it a mother and her child dead, and the father, with three more, living, but so much reduced by famine as to be unable to remove themselves from the flames. We carried them into the open air, and offered the old man our few remaining crumbs of biscuit, but he told us that he was too far gone to benefit by them, and begged that we would give them to his children. We lost no time in examining such of the other houses as were yet safe to enter, and rescued many more individuals from one horrible death, probably to reserve them for another equally so, and more lingering, as we had nothing to give them, and marched at daylight the following morning.

Our post that night was one of terrific grandeur. The hills behind were in a blaze of light with the British camp-fires, as were those in our front with the French ones. Both hills were abrupt and lofty, not above eight hundred yards asunder, and we were in the burning village in the valley between. The roofs of houses every instant falling in, and the sparks and flames ascending to the clouds. The streets were strewed with the dying and the dead,—some had been murdered and some killed in action, which, together with the half-famished wretches whom we had saved from burning, contributed in making it a scene which was well-calculated to shake a stout heart, as was proved in the instance of one of our sentries, a well known " devil-may-care" sort of fellow.

I know not what appearances the burning rafters might have reflected on the neighbouring trees at the time, but he had not been long on his post before he came running into the piquet, and swore, by all the saints in the calendar, that he saw six dead Frenchmen advancing upon him with hatchets over their shoulders!

We found by the buttons on the coats of some of the fallen foe, that we had this day been opposed to the French ninty-fifth regiment, (the same number as we were then,) and I cut off several of them, which I preserved as trophies.

March 15th.—We overtook the enemy a little before dark this afternoon. They were drawn up behind the Ceira, at Fez D'Aronce, with their rear-guard, under Marshal Ney, imprudently posted on our side of the river, a circumstance which Lord Wellington took immediate advantage of; and, by a furious attack, dislodged them, in such confusion, that they blew up the bridge before half of their own people had time to get over. Those who were thereby left behind, not choosing to put themselves to the pain of being shot, took to the river, which received them so hospitably that few of them ever quitted it. Their loss, on this occasion, must have been very great, and, we understood, at the time, that Ney had been sent to France, in disgrace, in consequence of it.

About the middle of the action, I observed some inexperienced light troops rushing up a deep road-way to certain destruction, and ran to warn them out of it, but I only arrived in time to partake the reward of their indiscretion, for I was instantly struck with a musket-ball above the left ear, which deposited me, at full length, in the mud.

I know not how long I lay insensible, but, on recovering, my first *feeling* was for my head, to ascertain if any part of it was still standing, for it appeared to me as if nothing remained above the mouth ; but, after repeated applications of all my fingers and thumbs to the doubtful parts, I, at length, proved to myself, satisfactorily, that it had rather increased than diminished by the concussion; and, jumping on my legs, and hearing, by the whistling of the balls from both sides, that the rascals who had got me into the scrape had been driven back and left me there, I snatched my cap, which had saved my life, and which had been spun off my head to the distance of ten or twelve yards, and joined them, a short distance in the rear, when one of them, a soldier of the sixtieth, came and told me that an officer of ours had been killed, a short time before, pointing to the spot where I myself had fallen, and that he had tried to take his jacket off, but that the advance of the enemy had prevented him. I told him that I was the one that had been killed, and that I was deucedly obliged to him for his *kind* intentions, while I felt still more so to the enemy for their timely advance, otherwise, I have no doubt, but my *friend* would have taken a fancy to my trousers also, for I found that he had absolutely unbuttoned my jacket.

There is nothing so gratifying to frail mortality as a good dinner when most wanted and least expected. It was perfectly dark before the action finished, but, on going to take advantage of the fires which the enemy had evacuated, we found their soup-kettles in full operation, and every man's mess of biscuit lying beside them, in stockings, as was the French mode of carrying them; and it is needless to say how unceremoniously we proceeded to do the honours of the feast. It ever after became a saying among the soldiers, whenever they were on short allowance, " well, d—n my eyes, we must either fall in with the French or the commissary to-day, I don't care which."

As our baggage was always in the rear on occasions of this kind, the officers of each company had a Portuguese boy, in charge of a donkey, on whom their little comforts depended. He carried our boat-cloaks and blankets, was provided with a small pig-skin for wine, a canteen for spirits, a small quantity of tea and sugar, a goat tied to the donkey, and two or three dollars in his pocket, for the purchase of bread, butter, or any other luxury which good fortune might throw in his way in the course of the day's march. We were never very scrupulous in exacting information regarding the source of his supplies; so that he had nothing to dread from our wrath, unless he had the misfortune to make his appearance empty-handed. They were singularly faithful and intelligent in making their way to us every evening, under the most difficult circumstances. This was the only night during Massena's retreat in which ours failed to find us; and, wandering the greater part of the night in the intricate maze of camp-fires, it appeared that he slept, after all, among some dragoons, within twenty yards of us.

CHAP. VI.

Passage of the Mondego. Swearing to a large Amount.
Two Prisoners, with their Two Views. Two Nuns, Two
Pieces of Dough, and Two Kisses. A Halt. Affair near
Frexedas. Arrival near Guarda. Murder. A stray
Sentry. Battle of Sabugal. Spanish and Portuguese
Frontiers. Blockade of Almeida. Battle-like. Current
Value of Lord Wellington's Nose. Battle of Fuentes
D'Onor. The Day after the Battle. A grave Remark.
The *Padre's* House. Retreat of the Enemy.

March 17th.—FOUND the enemy's rear-guard
behind the Mondego, at Ponte de Marcella,
cannonaded them out of it, and then threw a
temporary bridge across the river, and followed
them until dark.

The late Sir Alexander Campbell, who commanded the division next to ours, by a wanton

excess of zeal in expecting an order to follow, would not permit any thing belonging to us to pass the bridge, for fear of impeding the march of his troops ; and, as he received no order to march, we were thereby prevented from getting any thing whatever to eat for the next thirty-six hours. I know not whether the curses of individuals are recorded under such circumstances, but, if they are, the gallant general will have found the united hearty ones of four thousand men registered against him for that particular act.

March 19th.—We, this day, captured the aide-de-camp of General Loison, together with his wife, who was dressed in a splendid hussar uniform. *He* was a Portuguese, and a traitor, and looked very like a man who would be hanged. *She* was a Spaniard, and very handsome, and looked very like a woman who would get married again.

March 20th.—We had now been three days without any thing in the shape of bread, and meat without it, after a time, becomes almost loathsome. Hearing that we were not likely to march quite so early as usual this morning, I started, before daylight, to a village about two miles off, in the face of the Sierra D'Estrella, in the hopes of being able to purchase something, as it lay out of the hostile line of movements. On my arrival there, I found some nuns who had fled from a neighbouring convent, waiting outside the building of the village-oven for some Indian-corn-leaven, which they had carried there to be baked, and, when I explained my pressing wants, two of them, very kindly, transferred me their shares, for which I gave each a kiss and a dollar between. They took the former as an unusual favour; but looked at the latter, as much as to say, " our poverty, and not our will, consents." I ran off with my half-baked dough, and joined my comrades, just as they were getting under arms.

March 21st.—We, this day, reached the town of Mello, and had so far outmarched our commissary that we found it necessary to wait for him; and, in stopping to get a sight of our friends, we lost sight of our foes, a circumstance which I was by no means sorry for, as it enabled my shoulders, once more, to rejoice under the load of a couple of biscuits, and made me no longer ashamed to look a cow or a sheep in the face, now that they were not required to furnish more than their regulated proportions of my daily food.

March 30th.—We had no difficulty in tracing the enemy, by the wrecks of houses and the butchered peasantry; and overtook their rear-guard, this day, busy grinding corn, in some windmills, near the village of Frexedas. As their situation offered a fair opportunity for us to reap the fruits of their labours, we immediately attacked and drove them from it, and, after securing what we wanted, we withdrew again, across the valley, to the village of Alverca, where we were not without some reasonable expectations that they would have returned the compliment, as we had only a few squadrons of dragoons in addition to our battalion, and we had seen them withdraw a much stronger force from the opposite village; but, by keeping a number of our men all night employed in making extensive fires on the hill above, it induced them to think that our force was much greater than it really was; and we remained unmolested.

The only person we had hit in this affair was our adjutant, Mr. Stewart, who was shot through the head from a window. He was a gallant soldier, and deeply lamented. We placed his body in a chest, and buried it in front of Colonel Beckwith's quarters.

March 31st.—At daylight, this morning, we moved to our right, along the ridge of mountains, to Guarda: on our arrival there, we saw the imposing spectacle of the whole of the French army winding through the valley below, just out of gun-shot.

On taking possession of one of the villages which they had just evacuated, we found the body of a well-dressed female, whom they had murdered by a horrible refinement in cruelty. She had been placed upon her back, alive, in the middle of the street, with the fragment of a rock upon her breast, which it required four of our men to remove.

April 1st.—We overtook the enemy this afternoon, in position, behind the Coa, at Sabugal, with their advanced posts on our side of the river.

I was sent on piquet for the night, and had my sentries within half-musket shot of theirs: it was wet, dark, and stormy when I went, about midnight, to visit them, and I was not a little annoyed to find one missing. Recollecting who he was, a steady old soldier and the last man in the world to desert his post, I called his name aloud, when his answering voice, followed by the discharge of a musket, reached me nearly at the same time, from the direction of one of the French sentries; and, after some inquiry, I found that in walking his lonely round, in a brown study, no doubt, he had each turn taken ten or twelve paces to his front, and only half that number to the rear, until he had gradually worked himself up to within a few yards of his adversary; and it would be difficult to say which of the two was most astonished—the one at hearing a voice, or the other a shot so near, but all my rhetoric, aided by the testimony of the serjeant and the other sentries, could not convince the fellow that he was not on the identical spot on which I had posted him.

April 2d.—We moved this day to the right, nearer to the bridge, and some shots were exchanged between the piquets.

BATTLE OF SABUGAL.

April 3d, 1811.

Early this morning our division moved still farther to its right, and our brigade led the way across a ford, which took us up to the middle ; while the balls from the enemy's advanced posts were hissing in the water around us, we drove in their light troops and commenced a furious assault upon their main body. Thus far all was right; but a thick drizzling rain now came on, in consequence of which the third division, which was to have made a simultaneous attack to our left, missed their way, and a brigade of dragoons under Sir William Erskine, who were to have covered our right, went the Lord knows where, but certainly not into the fight, although they started at the same time that we did, and had the *music* of our rifles to guide them; and, even the second brigade of our own division could not afford us any support, for nearly an hour, so that we were thus unconsciously left with about fifteen hundred men, in the very impertinent attempt to carry a formidable position, on which stood as many thousands.

The weather, which had deprived us of the aid of our friends, favoured us so far as to prevent the enemy from seeing the amount of our paltry force; and the conduct of our gallant fellows, led on by Sir Sidney Beckwith, was so truly heroic, that, incredible as it may seem, we had the best of the fight throughout. Our first attack was met by such overwhelming numbers, that we were forced back and followed by three heavy columns, before which we retired slowly, and keeping up a destructive fire, to the nearest rising ground, where we reformed and instantly charged their advancing masses, sending them flying at the point of the bayonet, and entering their position along with them, where we were assailed by fresh forces. Three times did the very same thing occur. In our third attempt we got possession of one of their howitzers, for which a desperate struggle was making, when we were at the same moment charged by infantry in front and cavalry on the right, and again compelled to fall back; but, fortunately, at this moment we were reinforced by the arrival of the second brigade, and, with their aid, we once more stormed their position and secured the well-earned howitzer, while the third division came at the same time upon their flank, and they were driven from the field in the greatest disorder.

Lord Wellington's despatch on this occasion did ample justice to Sir Sidney Beckwith and his brave brigade. Never were troops more judiciously or more gallantly led. Never was a leader more devotedly followed.

In the course of the action a man of the name of Knight fell dead at my feet, and though I heard a musket ball strike him, I could neither find blood nor wound.

There was a little spaniel belonging to one of our officers running about the whole time, barking at the balls, and I saw him once smelling at a live shell, which exploded in his face without hurting him.

The strife had scarcely ended among mortals, when it was taken up by the elements with terrific violence. The *Scotch mist* of the morning had now increased to torrents, enough to cool the fever of our late excitement, and accompanied by thunder and lightning. As a compliment for our exertions in the fight, we were sent into the town, and had the advantage of whatever cover its dilapidated state afforded. While those who had not had the chance of getting broken skins, had now the benefit of sleeping in wet ones.

On the 5th of April we entered the frontiers of Spain, and slept in a bed for the first time since I left the ship. Passing from the Portuguese to the Spanish frontier is about equal to taking one step from the coal-hole into the parlour, for the cottages on the former are reared with filth, furnished with ditto, and peopled accordingly; whereas, those of Spain, even within the same mile, are neatly whitewashed, both without and within, and the poorest of them can furnish a good bed, with clean linen, and the pillow-cases neatly adorned with pink and sky-blue ribbons, while their dear little girls look smiling and neat as their pillow-cases.

After the action at Sabugal, the enemy retired to the neighbourhood of Ciudad Rodrigo, without our getting another look at them, and we took up the line of the Agueda and Axava rivers, for the blockade of the fortress of Almeida, in which they had left a garrison indifferently provisioned.

The garrison had no means of providing for their cattle, but by turning them out to graze upon the glacis; and we sent a few of our

rifles to practice against them, which very soon
reduced them to salt provisions.

Towards the end of April the French army
began to assemble on the opposite bank of the
Agueda to attempt the relief of the garrison,
while ours began to assemble in position at
Fuentes d'Onor to dispute it.

Our division still continued to hold the same
line of outposts, and had several sharp affairs
between the piquets at the bridge of Ma-
rialva.

As a general action seemed now to be inevitable, we anxiously longed for the return of Lord
Wellington, who had been suddenly called
to the corps of the army under Marshal
Beresford, near Badajos, as we would rather
see his long nose in the fight than a re-
inforcement of ten thousand men any day. Indeed, there was a charm not only about himself
but all connected with him, for which no odds
could compensate. The known abilities of Sir
George Murray, the gallant bearing of the

lamented Pakenham, of Lord Fitzroy Somerset, of the present Duke of Richmond, Sir Colin Campbell, with others, the flower of our young nobility and gentry, who, under the auspices of such a chief, seemed always a group attendant on victory; and I'll venture to say that there was not a bosom in that army that did not beat more lightly, when it heard the joyful news of his arrival, the day before the enemy's advance.

He had ordered us not to dispute the passage of the river, so that when the French army advanced, on the morning of the 3d of May, we retired slowly before them, across the plains of Espeja, and drew into the position, where the whole army was now assembled. Our division took post in reserve, in the left centre. Towards evening, the enemy made a fierce attack on the Village of Fuentes, but were repulsed with loss.

On the 4th, both armies looked at each other all day without exchanging shots.

E

BATTLE OF FUENTES D'ONOR,
May 5th, 1811.

The day began to dawn, this fine May morning, with a rattling fire of musketry on the extreme right of our position, which the enemy had attacked, and to which point our division was rapidly moved.

Our battalion was thrown into a wood, a little to the left and front of the division engaged, and was instantly warmly opposed to the French skirmishers; in the course of which I was struck with a musket-ball on the left breast, which made me stagger a yard or two backward, and, as I felt no pain, I concluded that I was dangerously wounded; but it turned out to be owing to my not being hurt. While our operations here were confined to a tame skirmish, and our view to the oaks with which we were mingled, we found, by the evidence of our ears, that the division which we had come to support was involved in a more serious onset, for *there* was the successive rattle of artillery, the wild hurrah of charging squadrons, and the repulsing volley of musketry; until Lord Wellington, finding his right too much extended, directed *that* division to fall back behind the small river Touronne, and ours to join the main body of the army. The execution of our movement presented a magnificent military spectacle, as the plain, between us and the right of the army, was by this time in possession of the French cavalry, and, while we were retiring through it with the order and precision of a common field-day, they kept dancing around us, and every instant threatening a charge, without daring to execute it.

We took up our new position at a right angle with the then right of the British line, on which our left rested, and with our right on the Touronne. The enemy followed our movement with a heavy column of infantry; but, when they came near enough to exchange shots, they did not seem to like our looks, as we occupied a low ridge of broken rocks, against which even a rat could scarcely have hoped to advance alive;

and they again fell back, and opening a tremendous fire of artillery, which was returned by a battery of our guns. In the course of a short time, seeing no further demonstration against this part of the position, our division was withdrawn, and placed in reserve in rear of the centre.

The battle continued to rage with fury in and about the village, whilst we were lying by our arms under a burning hot sun, some stray cannon-shot passing over and about us, whose progress we watched for want of other employment. One of them bounded along in the direction of an *amateur*, whom we had for some time been observing securely placed, as he imagined, behind a piece of rock, which stood about five feet above the ground, and over which nothing but his head was shown, sheltered from the sun by an umbrella. The shot in question touched the ground three or four times between us and him ; he saw it coming—lowered his umbrella, and withdrew his head. Its expiring bound carried it into the very spot where he had that instant disappeared. I hope he was not hurt; but the thing looked so ridiculous that it excited a shout of laughter, and we saw no more of him.

A little before dusk, in the evening, our battalion was ordered forward to relieve the troops engaged in the village, part of which still remained in possession of the enemy, and I saw, by the mixed nature of the dead, in every part of the streets, that it had been successively in possession of both sides. The firing ceased with the daylight, and I was sent, with a section of men, in charge of one of the streets for the night. There was a wounded serjeant of highlanders lying on my post. A ball had passed through the back part of his head, from which the brain was oozing, and his only sign of life was a convulsive hiccough every two or three seconds. I sent for a medical friend to look at him, who told me that he could not survive; I then got a mattress from the nearest house, placed the poor fellow on it, and made use of one corner as a pillow for myself, on which, after the fatigues of the day, and though called occasionally to visit my sentries, I slept most soundly. The highlander died in the course of the night.

When we stood to our arms, at daybreak next morning, we found the enemy busy throwing up a six-gun battery, immediately in front of our company's post, and we immediately set to work, with our whole hearts and souls, and placed a wall, about twelve feet thick, between us, which, no doubt, still remains there in the same garden, as a monument of what can be effected, in a few minutes, by a hundred modern men, when their personal safety is concerned; not but that the proprietor, in the midst of his admiration, would rather see a good bed of garlic on the spot, manured with the bodies of the architects.

When the sun began to shine on the pacific disposition of the enemy, we proceeded to consign the dead to their last earthly mansions, giving every Englishman a grave to himself, and putting as many Frenchmen into one as it could conveniently accommodate. Whilst in the superintendence of this melancholy duty, and ruminating on the words of the poet:—

" There's not a form of all that lie
    Thus ghastly, wild and bare,
  Tost, bleeding, in the stormy sky,
    Black in the burning air,
  But to his knee some infant clung,
  But on his heart some fond heart hung! "

I was grieved to think that the souls of deceased warriors should be so selfish as to take to flight in their regimentals, for I never saw the body of one with a rag on after battle.

The day after one of those negative sort of victories is always one of intense interest. The movements on each side are most jealously watched, and each side is diligently occupied in strengthening such points as the fight of the preceding day had proved to be the most vulnerable.

Lord Wellington was too deficient in his cavalry force to justify his following up his victory;

and the enemy, on their parts, had been too roughly handled, in their last attempt, to think of repeating the experiment; so that, during the next two days, though both armies continued to hold the same ground, there was scarcely a shot exchanged.

They had made a few prisoners, chiefly guardsmen and highlanders, whom they marched past the front of our position, in the most ostentatious way, on the forenoon of the 6th; and, the day following, a number of their regiments were paraded in the most imposing manner for review. They looked uncommonly well, and we were proud to think that we had beaten such fine-looking fellows so lately!

Our regiment had been so long and so often quartered in Fuentes that it was like fighting for our fire-sides. The *Padre's* house stood at the top of the town. He was an old friend of ours, and an old fool, for he would not leave his house until it was too late to take anything with him; but, curious enough, although it had been repeatedly in the possession of both sides, and plundered, no doubt, by many expert artists, yet none of them thought of looking so high as the garret, which happened to be the repository of his money and provisions. He came to us the day after the battle, weeping over his supposed loss, like a sensitive Christian, and I accompanied him to the house, to see whether there was not some consolation remaining for him; but, when he found his treasure safe, he could scarcely bear its restoration with becoming gravity. I helped him to carry off his bag of dollars, and he returned the compliment with a leg of mutton.

The French army retired on the night of the 7th, leaving Almeida to its fate; but, by an extraordinary piece of luck, the garrison made their escape the night after, in consequence of some mistake or miscarriage of an order, which prevented a British regiment from occupying the post intended for it.

May 8th.—We advanced this morning, and occupied our former post at Espeja, with some hopes of remaining quiet for a few days; but the alarm sounding at daylight on the following morning, we took post on the hill, in front of the village. It turned out to be only a patrole of French cavalry, who retired on receiving a few shots from our piquets, and we saw no more of them for a considerable time.

CHAP. VII.

March to Estremadura. At Soito, growing Accommodations for Man and Beast. British Taste displayed by Portuguese Wolves. False Alarm. Luxuries of Roquingo Camp. A Chaplain of the Forces. Return towards the North. Quarters near Castello de Vide. Blockade of Ciudad Rodrigo. Village of Atalya ; Fleas abundant ; Food scarce. Advance of the French Army. Affairs near Guinaldo. Our Minister administered to. An unexpected Visit from our General and his Followers. End of the Campaign of 1811. Winter Quarters.

LORD WELLINGTON, soon after the battle of Fuentes, was again called into Estremadura, to superintend the operations of the corps of the army under Marshal Beresford, who had, in the mean time, fought the battle of Albuera, and laid siege to Badajos. In the beginning of June our division was ordered thither also, to be in readiness to aid his operations. We halted one night at the village of Soito, where there are a great many chestnut trees of very extraordinary dimensions; the outside of the trunk keeps growing as the inside decays. I was one of a party of four persons who dined inside of one, and I saw two or three horses put up in several others.

We halted, also, one night on the banks of the Coa, near Sabugal, and visited our late field of battle. We found that the dead had been nearly all torn from their graves, and devoured by wolves, who are in great force in that wild mountainous district, and shew very little respect either for man or beast. They seldom, indeed, attack a man; but if one happens to tie his horse to a tree, and leaves him unattended, for a short time, he must not be surprised if he finds, on his return, that he has parted with a good *rump steak*; *that* is the piece that they always prefer ; and it is, therefore, clear to me, that the first of the wolves must have been reared in England !

We experienced, in the course of this very dark night, one of those ridiculous false alarms which will sometimes happen in the best organized body. Some bullocks strayed, by accident, amongst the piles of arms, the falling clatter of which, frightened them so much that they went galloping over the sleeping soldiers. The officers' baggage-horses broke from their *moorings,* and joined in the general charge ; and a cry immediately arose, that it was the French cavalry. The different regiments stood to their arms, and formed squares, looking as sharp as thunder for something to fire at; and it was a considerable time before the cause of the *row* could be traced. The different followers of the army, in the mean time, were scampering off to the rear, spreading the most frightful reports. One woman of the 52d succeeded in getting three leagues off before day-light, and swore, " that, as God was her judge, she did not leave her regiment until she saw the last man of them cut to pieces ! ! !"

On our arrival near Elvas, we found that Marshal Beresford had raised the siege of Badajos; and we were, therefore, encamped on the river Caya, near Roquingo. This was a sandy unsheltered district; and the weather was so excessively hot, that we had no enjoyment, but that of living three parts of the day up to the neck in a pool of water.

Up to this period it had been a matter of no small difficulty to ascertain, at any time, the day of the week; that of the month was altogether out of the question, and could only be reckoned by counting back to the date of the last battle; but our division was here joined by a chaplain, whose duty it was to remind us of these things. He might have been a very good man, but he was not prepossessing, either in his appearance or manners. I remember, the first Sunday after his arrival, the troops were paraded for divine service, and had been some time waiting in square, when he at length rode

into the centre of it, with his tall, lank, un-
gainly figure, mounted on a starved, untrim-
med, unfurnished horse, and followed by a
Portuguese boy, with his canonicals and prayer-
books on the back of a mule, with a hay-
bridle, and having, by way of clothing, about
half a pair of straw breeches. This spiritual
comforter was the least calculated of any one
that I ever saw to excite devotion in the minds
of men, who had seen nothing in the shape of
a divine for a year or two.

In the beginning of August we began to
retrace our steps towards the north. We halted
a few days in Portalegre, and a few more at
Castello de Vide.

The latter place is surrounded by extensive
gardens, belonging to the richer citizens; in
each of which there is a small summer-house,
containing one or two apartments, in which the
proprietor, as I can testify, may have the enjoyment of being fed upon by a more healthy and
better appetized flea, than is to be met with in
town houses in general.

These *quintas* fell to the lot of our battalion; and though their beds, on that account, had not much sleep in them, yet, as those who preferred the voice of the nightingale in a bed of cabbages, to the pinch of a flea in a bed of feathers, had the alternative at their option; I enjoyed my sojourn there very much. Each garden had a bathing tank, with a plentiful supply of water, which at that season was really a luxury; and they abounded in choice fruits. I there formed an attachment to a mulberry-tree, which is still fondly cherished in my remembrance.

We reached the scene of our former operations, in the north, towards the end of August.

The French had advanced and blockaded Almeida, during our absence, but they retired again on our approach, and we took up a more advanced position than before, for the blockade of Ciudad Rodrigo.

Our battalion occupied Atalya, a little village at the foot of the Sierra de Gata, and in front of the River Vadilla. On taking possession of my quarter, the people showed me an outhouse,

which, they said, I might use as a stable, and
I took my horse into it, but, seeing the floor
strewed with what appeared to be a small brown
seed, heaps of which lay in each corner, as if
shovelled together in readiness to take to mar-
ket, I took up a handful, out of curiosity, and,
truly, they were a curiosity, for I found that
they were all regular fleas, and that they were
proceeding to eat both me and my horse, without
the smallest ceremony. I rushed out of the
place, and knocked them down by fistfuls, and
never yet could comprehend the cause of their
congregating together in such a place.

This neighbourhood had been so long the
theatre of war, and alternately forced to supply
both armies, that the inhabitants, at length,
began to dread starvation themselves, and concealed, for their private use, all that remained
to them; so that, although they were bountiful
in their assurances of good wishes, it was impossible to extract a loaf of their good bread, of
which we were so wildly in want that we were
obliged to conceal patroles on the different roads

and footpaths, for many miles around, to search
the peasants passing between the different villages, giving them an order on the commissary
for whatever we took from them; and we were
not too proud to take even a few potatoes out of
an old woman's basket.

On one occasion, when some of us were out
shooting, we discovered about twenty hives of
bees, in the face of a glen, concealed among the
gumcestus, and, stopping up the mouth of one
them, we carried it home on our shoulders, bees
and all, and continued to levy contributions on
the *depot* as long as we remained there.

Towards the end of September, the garrison
of Ciudad Rodrigo began to get on such "short
commons" that *Marmont*, who had succeeded
Massena, in the command of the French army,
found it necessary to assemble the whole of his
forces, to enable him to throw provisions into it.

Lord Wellington was still pursuing his defensive system, and did not attempt to oppose him;
but Marmont, after having effected his object,
thought that he might as well take that opportu-

nity of beating up our quarters, in return for the trouble we had given him; and, accordingly, on the morning of the 25th, he attacked a brigade of the third division, stationed at El Bedon, which, after a brilliant defence and retreat, conducted him opposite to the British position, in front of Fuente Guinaldo. He busied himself, the whole of the following day, in bringing up his troops for the attack. Our division, in the mean time, remained on the banks of the Vadillo, and had nearly been cut off, through the obstinacy of General Crawford, who did not choose to obey an order he received to retire the day before; but we, nevertheless, succeeded in joining the army, by a circuitous route, on the afternoon of the 26th; and, the whole of both armies being now assembled, we considered a battle on the morrow as inevitable.

Lord Wellington, however, was not disposed to accommodate them on this occasion; for, about the middle of the night, we received an order to stand to our arms, with as little noise as possible, and to commence retiring, the rest

of the army having been already withdrawn,
unknown to us; an instance of the rapidity and
uncertainty of our movements which proved fatal
to the liberty of several amateurs and followers
of the army, who, seeing an army of sixty
thousand men lying asleep around their camp-
fires, at ten o'clock at night, naturally concluded
that they might safely indulge in a bed in the
village behind, until daylight, without the risk
of being caught napping; but, long ere that
time, they found themselves on the high road to
Ciudad Rodrigo, in the rude grasp of an enemy.
Amongst others, was the chaplain of our division,
whose outward man, as I have already said,
conveyed no very exalted notion of the respectability of his profession, and who was treated
with greater indignity than usually fell to the lot
of prisoners, for, after keeping him a couple of
days, and finding that, however gifted he might
have been in spiritual lore, he was as ignorant as Dominie Sampson on military matters ;
and, conceiving good provisions to be thrown
away upon him, they stripped him nearly naked

and dismissed him, like the barber in Gil Blas, with a kick in the breech, and sent him in to us in a woful state.

September 27th.—General Crawford remained behind us this morning, with a troop of dragoons, to reconnoitre; and, while we were marching carelessly along the road, he and his dragoons galloped right into our column, with a cloud of French ones at his heels. Luckily, the ground was in our favour; and, dispersing our men among the broken rocks, on both sides of the road, we sent them back somewhat faster than they came on. They were, however, soon replaced by their infantry, with whom we continued in an uninteresting skirmish all day. There was some sharp firing, the whole of the afternoon, to our left; and we retired, in the evening, to Soito.

This affair terminated the campaign of 1811, as the enemy retired the same night, and we advanced next day to resume the blockade of Rodrigo; and were suffered to remain quietly in cantonments until the commencement of a new year.

In every interval between our active services, we indulged in all manner of childish trick and amusement, with an avidity and delight of which it is impossible to convey an adequate idea. We lived united, as men always are who are daily staring death in the face on the same side, and who, caring little about it, look upon each new day added to their lives as one more to rejoice in.

We invited the villagers, every evening, to a dance at our quarters alternately. A Spanish peasant girl has an address about her which I have never met with in the same class of any other country; and she at once enters into society with the ease and confidence of one who had been accustomed to it all her life. We used to flourish away at the bolero, fandango, and waltz, and wound up early in the evening with a supper of roasted chestnuts.

Our village *belles*, as already stated, made themselves perfectly at home in our society, and we, too, should have enjoyed theirs for a season; but, when month after month, and year after year, continued to roll along, without producing any change, we found that the cherry cheek and sparkling eye of rustic beauty furnished but a very poor apology for the illuminated portion of Nature's fairest works, and ardently longed for an opportunity of once more feasting our eyes on a *lady*.

In the month of December, we heard that the chief magistrate of Rodrigo, with whom we were personally acquainted, had, with his daughter and two other young ladies, taken shelter in Robledillo, a little town in the Sierra de Gata, which, being within our range, presented an attraction not to be resisted.

Half-a-dozen of us immediately resolved ourselves into a committee of ways and means. We had six months' pay due to us; so that the fandango might have been danced in either of our pockets without the smallest risk; but we had this consolation for our poverty, that there was nothing to be bought, even if we had the

means. Our only resource, therefore, was to
lighten the cares of such of our brother-officers
as were fortunate enough to have any thing to
lose; and, at this moment of doubt and difficulty,
a small flock of turkeys, belonging to our major,
presented themselves, most imprudently, grazing
opposite the windows of our council-chamber,
two of which were instantly committed to the
bottom of a sack, as a foundation to go upon.
One of our spies, soon after, apprehended a
sheep, the property of another officer, which
was committed to the same place; and, getting
the commissary to advance us a few extra loaves
of bread, some ration beef, and a pig-skin full
of wine, we placed a servant on a mule, with
the whole concern tackled to him, and proceeded
on our journey.

In passing over the mountain, we saw a wild
boar bowling along, in the midst of a snow-storm,
and, voting them fitting companions, we suffered
him to pass, (particularly as he did not come
within shot).

On our arrival at Robledillo, we met with the

most cordial reception from the old magistrate ; who, entering into the spirit of our visit, provided us with quarters, and filled our room in the evening with every body worth seeing in the place. We were malicious enough, by way of amusement, to introduce a variety of absurd pastimes, under the pretence of their being English, and which, by virtue thereof, were implicitly adopted. We, therefore, passed a regular romping evening ; and, at a late hour, having conducted the ladies to their homes, some friars, who were of the party, very kindly, intended doing us the same favour, and, with that view, had begun to precede us with their lanterns, but, in the frolic of the moment, we set upon them with snow-balls, some of which struck upon their broad shoulders, while others fizzed against their fiery faces, and, in their astonishment and alarm, all sanctimony was forgotten ; their oaths flew as thick as our snow-balls, while they ran ducking their heads and dousing their lights, for better concealment; but we, nevertheless, persevered until we had pelted each to his own home.

F

We were, afterwards, afraid that we had carried the joke rather too far, and entertained some doubts as to the propriety of holding our quarters for another day; but they set our minds at rest on that point, by paying us an early visit in the morning, and seemed to enjoy the joke in a manner that we could not have expected from the gravity of their looks.

We passed two more days much in the same manner, and, on the third, returned to our cantonments, and found that our division had moved, during our absence, into some villages nearer to Ciudad Rodrigo, preparatory to the siege of that place.

On inquiry, we found that we had never been suspected for the *abduction* of the sheep and turkeys, but that the blame, on the contrary, had been attached to the poor soldiers, whose soup had been tasted every day to see if it savoured of such dainties. The proprietor of the turkeys was so particularly indignant that we thought it prudent not to acknowledge ourselves as the culprits until some time afterwards, when, as one of our party happened to be killed in action, we, very uncharitably, put the whole of it on his shoulders.

CHAP. VIII.

Siege of Ciudad Rodrigo. The Garrison of an Outwork relieved. Spending an Evening abroad. A Musical Study. An Addition to Soup. A short Cut. Storming of the Town. A sweeping Clause. Advantages of leading a Storming Party. Looking for a Customer. Disadvantages of being a stormed Party. Confusion of all Parties. A waking Dream. Death of General Crawford. Accident. Deaths.

SIEGE OF CIUDAD RODRIGO,

January 8th, 1812.

THE campaign of 1812 commenced with the siege of Ciudad Rodrigo, which was invested by our division on the 8th of January.

There was a smartish frost, with some snow on the ground; and, when we arrived opposite the fortress, about midday, the garrison did not appear to think that we were in earnest, for a number of their officers came out, under the shelter of a stone-wall, within half musket-shot, and amused themselves in saluting and bowing to us in ridicule ; but, ere the day was done, some of them had occasion to wear the laugh on the opposite side of the countenance.

We lay by our arms until dark, when a party, consisting of a hundred volunteers from each regiment, under Colonel Colborne, of the fifty-second, stormed and carried the Fort of St. Francisco, after a short sharp action, in which the whole of its garrison were taken or destroyed. The officer who commanded it was a chattering little fellow, and acknowledged himself to have been one of our saluting friends of the morning. He kept, incessantly, repeating a few words of English which he had picked up during the assault, and the only ones, I fancy, that were spoken, viz. " dem eyes, b—t eyes!" and, in demanding the meaning of them, he required that we should, also, explain why we stormed a place without first besieging it ; for, he said, that another officer would have relieved him of his charge at daylight, had *we* not *relieved* him of it sooner.

The enemy had calculated that this outwork would have kept us at bay for a fortnight or three weeks; whereas, its capture, the first night, enabled us to break ground at once, within breaching distance of the walls of the town. They kept up a very heavy fire the whole night on the working parties ; but, as they aimed at random, we did not suffer much ; and made such good use of our time that, when daylight enabled them to see what we were doing, we had dug ourselves under tolerable cover.

In addition to ours, the first, third, and fourth divisions were employed in the siege. Each took the duties for twenty-four hours alternately, and returned to their cantonments during the interval.

We were relieved by the first division, under Sir Thomas Graham, on the morning of the 9th, and marched to our quarters.

Jan. 12th.—At ten o'clock this morning we resumed the duties of the siege. It still continued to be dry frosty weather; and, as we were obliged to ford the Agueda, up to the middle, every man carried a pair of iced breeches into the trenches with him.

My turn of duty did not arrive until eight in the evening, when I was ordered to take thirty men with shovels to dig holes for ourselves, as near as possible to the walls, for the delectable amusement of firing at the embrazures for the remainder of the night. The enemy threw frequent fire-balls among us, to see where we were; but, as we always lay snug until their blaze was extinguished, they were not much the wiser, except by finding, from having some one popt off from their guns every instant, that they had got some neighbours whom they would have been glad to get rid of.

We were relieved as usual at ten next morning, and returned to our cantonments.

January 16th.—Entered on our third day's duty, and found the breaching batteries in full operation, and our approaches close to the walls on every side. When we arrived on the ground I was sent to take command of the highland company, which we had at that time in the regiment, and which was with the left wing, under Colonel Cameron. I found them on piquet, between the right of the trenches and the river, half of them posted at a mud-cottage, and the other half in a ruined convent, close under the walls. It was a very tolerable post when at it; but it is no joke travelling by daylight up to within a stone's throw of a wall, on which there is a parcel of fellows who have no other amusement but to fire at every body they see.

We could not show our noses at any point without being fired at; but, as we were merely posted there to protect the right flank of the trenches from any sortie, we did not fire at them, and kept as quiet as could be, considering the deadly blast that was blowing around us. There are few situations in life where something cannot be learnt, and I, myself, stand indebted to my twenty-four hours' residence there, for a more correct knowledge of martial sounds than in the study of my whole life time besides. They must be an unmusical pair of ears that cannot inform the wearer whither a cannon or a musket played last, but the various *notes*, emanating from their respective mouths, admit of nice distinctions. My party was too small, and too well sheltered to repay the enemy for the expense of shells and round shot; but the quantity of grape and musketry aimed at our particular heads, made a good concert of first and second whistles, while the more sonorous voice of the round shot, travelling to our friends on the left, acted as a thorough bass; and there was not a shell, that passed over us to the trenches, that did not send back a fragment among us as soon as it burst, as if to gratify a curiosity that I was far from expressing.

We went into the cottage soon after dark, to partake of something that had been prepared for dinner; and, when in the middle of it, a round shot passed through both walls, immediately over our heads, and garnished the soup with a greater quantity of our parent earth than was quite palatable.

We were relieved, as usual, by the first division, at ten next morning; and, to avoid as much as possible the destructive fire from the walls, they sent forward only three or four men at a time, and we sent ours away in the same proportions.

Every thing is by comparison in this world, and it is curious to observe how men's feelings change with circumstances. In cool blood a man would rather go a little out of his way than expose himself to unnecessary danger; but we found, this morning, that by crossing the river where we then were, and running the gauntlet for a mile, exposed to the fire of two pieces of artillery, that we should be saved the distance of two or three miles in returning to our quarters. After coming out of such a *furnace* as we had been frying in, the other fire was not considered a fire at all, and passed without a moment's hesitation.

STORMING OF CIUDAD RODRIGO.

January 19th, 1812.—We moved to the scene of operations, about two o'clock this afternoon; and, as it was a day before our regular turn, we concluded that we were called there to lend a hand in finishing the job we had begun so well; nor were we disappointed, for we found that two practicable breaches had been effected, and that the place was to be stormed in the evening by the third and light divisions, the former by the right breach, and the latter by the left, while some Portuguese troops were to attempt an escalade on the opposite sides of the town.

About eight o'clock in the evening our division was accordingly formed for the assault, behind a convent, near the left breach, in the following order:—viz.

1st. Four companies of our battalion, under Colonel Cameron, to line the crest of the glacis, and fire upon the ramparts.

2d. Some companies of Portuguese, carrying bags filled with hay and straw, for throwing into the ditch, to facilitate the passage of the storming party.

3d. The *forlorn hope*, consisting of an officer and twenty-five volunteers.

4th. The *storming party*, consisting of three officers and one hundred volunteers from each regiment, the officers from ours were Captain Mitchell, Mr. Johnstone, and myself, and the whole under the command of Major Napier, of the fifty-second.

5th. The main body of the division, under General Crawford, with one brigade, under Major-General Vandeleur, and the other under Colonel Barnard.

At a given signal the different columns advanced to the assault; the night was tolerably clear, and the enemy evidently expected us; for,

as soon as we turned the corner of the convent-
wall, the space between us and the breach became one blaze of light with their fire-balls,
which, while they lighted us on to glory, lightened not a few of their lives and limbs; for the
whole glacis was in consequence swept by a
well directed fire of grape and musketry, and
they are the devil's own brooms ; but our gallant
fellows walked through it, to the point of attack,
with the most determined steadiness, excepting
the Portuguese sack-bearers, most of whom lay
down behind their bags, to wait the result, while
the few that were thrown into the ditch looked
so like dead bodies, that, when I leapt into it, I
tried to avoid them.

The advantage of being on a storming party
is considered as giving the prior claim to be
put out of pain, for they receive the first
fire, which is generally the best, not to mention
that they are also expected to receive the earliest
salutation from the beams of timber, hand-
grenades, and other missiles, which the garrison
are generally prepared to transfer from the top

of the wall, to the tops of the heads of their foremost visitors. But I cannot say that I, myself, experienced any such preference, for every ball has a considerable distance to travel, and I have generally found them equally ready to pick up their man at the end, as at the beginning of their flight; luckily, too, the other preparations cannot always be accommodated to the moment, so that, on the whole, the *odds* are pretty *even*, that, all concerned come in for an equal share of whatever happens to be going on.

We had some difficulty at first in finding the breach, as we had entered the ditch opposite to a ravelin, which we mistook for a bastion. I tried first one side of it and then the other, and seeing one corner of it a good deal battered, with a ladder placed against it, I concluded that it must be the breach, and calling to the soldiers near me, to follow. I mounted with the most ferocious intent, carrying a sword in one hand and a pistol in the other; but, when I got up, I found nobody to fight with, except two of our own men, who were already laid dead across the top of the ladder. I saw, in a moment, that I had got into the wrong box, and was about to descend again, when I heard a shout from the opposite side, that the breach was there ; and, moving in that direction, I dropped myself from the ravelin, and landed in the ditch, opposite to the foot of the breach, where I found the head of the storming party just beginning to fight their way into it. The combat was of short duration, and, in less than half an hour from the commencement of the attack, the place was in our possession.

After carrying the breach, we met with no further opposition, and moved round the ramparts to see that they were perfectly clear of the enemy, previous to entering the town. I was fortunate enough to take the left-hand circuit, by accident, and thereby escaped the fate which befel a great portion of those who went to the right, and who were blown up, along with some of the third division, by the accidental explosion of a magazine.

I was highly amused, in moving round the ramparts, to find some of the Portuguese troops just commencing their escalade, on the opposite side, near the bridge, in ignorance of the place having already fallen.   Gallantly headed by their officers, they had got some ladders placed against the wall, while about two thousand voices from the rear were cheering, with all their might, for mutual encouragement ; and, like most other troops, under similar circumstances, it appeared to me that their feet and their tongues went at a more equal pace after we gave them the hint.   On going a little further, we came opposite to the ravelin, which had been my chief annoyance during my last days' piquet. It was still crowded by the enemy, who had now thrown down their arms, and endeavoured to excite our pity by virtue of their being " Pauvres Italianos ;" but our men had, somehow, imbibed a horrible antipathy to the Italians, and every appeal they made in that name was invariably answered with, — " You're Italians, are you ? then, d—n you, here's a shot for you;" and the action instantly followed the word.

A town taken by storm presents a frightful scene of outrage. The soldiers no sooner obtain possession of it, than they think themselves at liberty to do what they please. It is enough for them that there *had* been an enemy on the ramparts; and, without considering that the poor inhabitants may, nevertheless, be friends and allies, they, in the first moment of excitement, all share one common fate; and nothing but the most extraordinary exertions on the part of the officers can bring them back to a sense of their duty.

We continued our course round the ramparts until we met the head of the column which had gone by the right, and then descended into the town. At the entrance of the first street, a French officer came out of a door and claimed my protection, giving me his sword. He told me that there was another officer in the same house who was afraid to venture out, and entreated that I would go in for him. I, accordingly, fol-

lowed him up to the landing-place of a dark
stair, and, while he was calling to his friend, by
name, to come down, " as there was an English
officer present who would protect him," a violent
screaming broke through a door at my elbow. I
pushed it open, and found the landlady struggling with an English soldier, whom I immediately transferred to the bottom of the stair
head foremost. The French officer had followed
me in at the door, and was so astonished at all
he saw, that he held up his hands, turned up the
whites of his eyes, and resolved himself into a
state of the most eloquent silence. When he
did recover the use of his tongue, it was to
recommend his landlady to my notice, as the
most amiable woman in existence. She, on her
part, professed the most unbounded gratitude,
and entreated that I would make her house my
home for ever; but, when I called upon her, a
few days after, she denied having ever seen me
before, and stuck to it most religiously.

As the other officer could not be found, I
descended into the street again with my prisoner;

and, finding the current of soldiers setting
towards the centre of the town, I followed the
stream, which conducted me into the great
square, on one side of which the late garrison
were drawn up as prisoners, and the rest of it
was filled with British and Portuguese intermixed, without any order or regularity. I had
been there but a very short time, when they all
commenced firing, without any ostensible cause ;
some fired in at the doors and windows, some
at the roofs of houses, and others at the clouds ;
and, at last, some heads began to be blown
from their shoulders in the general hurricane,
when the voice of Sir Thomas Picton, with the
power of twenty trumpets, began to proclaim
damnation to every body, while Colonel Barnard, Colonel Cameron, and some other active
officers, were carrying it into effect with a strong
hand ; for, seizing the broken barrels of muskets,
which were lying about in great abundance, they
belaboured every fellow, most unmercifully,
about the head who attempted either to load or
fire, and finally succeeded in reducing them to

order. In the midst of the scuffle, however, three
of the houses in the square were set on fire; and
the confusion was such that nothing could be
done to save them; but, by the extraordinary
exertions of Colonel Barnard, during the whole
of the night, the flames were prevented from
communicating to the adjoining buildings.

We succeeded in getting a great portion of
our battalion together by one o'clock in the morning, and withdrew with them to the ramparts,
where we lay by our arms until daylight.

There is nothing in this life half so enviable
as the feelings of a soldier after a victory. Previous to a battle, there is a certain sort of something that pervades the mind which is not easily
defined; it is neither akin to joy or fear, and,
probably, *anxiety* may be nearer to it than any
other word in the dictionary: but, when the
battle is over, and crowned with victory, he finds
himself elevated for awhile into the regions of
absolute bliss! It had ever been the summit of
my ambition to attain a post at the head of a
storming party :—my wish had now been ac-

complished, and gloriously ended ; and I do think that, after all was over, and our men laid asleep on the ramparts, that I strutted about as important a personage, in my own opinion, as ever trod the face of the earth ; and, had the ghost of the renowned Jack-the-giant-killer itself passed that way at the time, I'll venture to say, that I would have given it a kick in the breech without the smallest ceremony. But, as the sun began to rise, I began to fall from the heroics ; and, when he showed his face, I took a look at my own, and found that I was too unclean a spirit to worship, for I was covered with mud and dirt, with the greater part of my dress torn to rags.

The fifth division, which had not been employed in the siege, marched in, and took charge of the town, on the morning of the 20th, and we prepared to return to our cantonments. Lord Wellington happened to be riding in at the gate at the time that we were marching out, and had the curiosity to ask the officer of the leading company, what regiment it was, for there was scarcely a vestige of uniform among the men, some of whom were dressed in Frenchmen's coats, some in white breeches, and huge jack-boots, some with cocked hats and queues; most of their swords were fixed on the rifles, and stuck full of hams, tongues, and loaves of bread, and not a few were carrying bird-cages! There never was a better masked corps!

General Crawford fell on the glacis, at the head of our division, and was buried at the foot of the breach which they so gallantly carried. His funeral was attended by Lord Wellington, and all the officers of the division, by whom he was, ultimately, much liked. He had introduced a system of discipline into the light division which made them unrivalled. A very rigid exaction of the duties pointed out in his code of regulations made him very unpopular at its commencement, and it was not until a short time before he was lost to us for ever, that we were capable of appreciating his merits, and fully sensible of the incalculable advantages we derived from the perfection of his system.

Among other things carried from Ciudad Rodrigo, one of our men had the misfortune to carry his death in his hands, under the mistaken shape of amusement. He thought that it was a cannon-ball, and took it for the purpose of playing at the game of nine-holes, but it happened to be a live shell. In rolling it along it went over a bed of burning ashes, and ignited without his observing it. Just as he had got it between his legs, and was in the act of discharging it a second time, it exploded, and nearly blew him to pieces.

Several men of our division, who had deserted while we were blockading Ciudad Rodrigo, were taken when it fell, and were sentenced to be shot. Lord Wellington extended mercy to every one who could procure any thing like a good character from his officers; but six of them, who could not, were paraded and shot, in front of the division, near the village of Ituera. Shooting appears to me to be a cruel kind of execution, for twenty balls may pierce a man's body without touching a vital spot. On the occasion alluded to, two of the men remained standing after the first fire, and the Provost-Marshal was obliged to put an end to their sufferings, by placing the muzzle of a piece at each of their heads.

CHAP. IX.

March to Estremadura. A Deserter shot. Riding for an Appetite. Effect the Cure of a sick Lady. Siege of Badajos. Trench-Work. Varieties during the Siege. Taste of the Times. Storming of the Town. Its Fall. Officers of a French Battalion. Not shot by Accident. Military Shopkeepers. Lost Legs and cold Hearts. Affecting Anecdote. My Servant. A Consignment to Satan. March again for the North. Sir Sidney Beckwith.

WE remained about six weeks in cantonments, after the fall of Ciudad Rodrigo; and, about the end of February, were again put in motion towards Estremadura.

March 7th.—Arrived near Castello de Vide, and quartered in the neighbouring villages. Another deserter, who had also been taken at the storming of Ciudad Rodrigo, was here shot,

under the sentence of a court martial. When
he was paraded for that purpose, he protested
against their right to shoot him, until he first
received the arrears of pay which was due at
the time of his desertion.

March 14th.—Two of us rode out this afternoon
to kill time until dinner hour (six); but, when we
returned to our quarters, there was not a vestige
of the regiment remaining, and our appetites
were considerably whetted, by having an additional distance of fourteen miles to ride, in the
dark, over roads on which we could not trust
our horses out of a walk. We joined them, at
about eleven at night, in the town of Portalegré.

March 16th.—Quartered in the town of Elvas.

I received a billet on a neat little house, occupied by an old lady and her daughter, who were
very desirous of evading such an incumbrance.
For, after resisting my entrance, until successive
applications of my foot had reduced the door to
a condition which would no longer second their
efforts, the old lady resolved to try me on another
tack; and, opening the door, and, making a sign

for me to make no noise, she told me, in a whisper, that her daughter was lying dangerously ill of a fever, in the only bed in the house, and that she was, therefore, excessively sorry that she could not accommodate me. As this information did not at all accord with my notions of consistency, after their having suffered the preceding half hour's bombardment, I requested to be shewn to the chamber of the invalid, saying that I was a *medico*, and might be of service to her. When she found remonstrance unavailing, she at length shewed me into a room up-stairs, where there was a very genteel-looking young girl, the very picture of *Portuguese* health, lying with her eyes shut, in full dress, on the top of the bed-clothes, where she had hurriedly thrown herself.

Seeing, at once, how matters stood, I walked up to the bed-side, and hit her a slap on the thigh with my hand, asking her, at the same time, how she felt herself? and never did Prince Hohenloe, himself, perform a miracle more cleverly; for she bounced almost as high as the

ceiling, and flounced about the room, as well
and as actively as ever she did, with a countenance in which shame, anger, and a great portion of natural humour were so amusingly
blended, that I was tempted to provoke her still
further by a salute. Having thus satisfied the
mother that I had been the means of restoring
her daughter to her usual state of health, she
thought it prudent to put the best face upon it,
and, therefore, invited me to partake of their
family dinner; in the course of which I succeeded so well in eating my way into their
affections, that we parted next morning with
mutual regret; they told me that I was the
best officer they had ever seen, and begged that
I would always make their house my home; but
I was never fated to see them again. We
marched in the morning for Badajos.

SIEGE OF BADAJOS.

On the 17th of March, 1812, the *third, fourth,*
and *light divisions,* encamped around Badajos,

embracing the whole of the inland side of the town on the left bank of the Guadiana, and commenced breaking ground before it immediately after dark the same night.

The elements, on this occasion, adopted the cause of the besieged; for we had scarcely taken up our ground, when a heavy rain commenced, and continued, almost without intermission, for a fortnight; in consequence thereof, the pontoon-bridge, connecting us with our supplies from Elvas, was carried away, by the rapid increase of the river, and the duties of the trenches were otherwise rendered extremely harassing. We had a smaller force employed than at Rodrigo; and the scale of operations was so much greater, that it required every man to be actually in the trenches six hours every day, and the same length of time every night, which, with the time required to march to and from them, through fields more than ankle deep in a stiff mud, left us never more than eight hours out of the twenty-four in camp, and we never were dry the whole time.

One day's trench-work is as like another as
the days themselves; and like nothing better
than serving an apprenticeship to the double
calling of grave-digger and game-keeper, for we
found ample employment both for the spade and
the rifle.

The only varieties during the siege were,—
First, The storming of *Picuvina*, a formidable
outwork, occupying the centre of our operations. It was carried one evening, in the most
gallant style, by Major-General Sir James
Kempt, at the head of the covering parties.
Secondly, A sortie made by the garrison, which
they got the worst of, although they succeeded
in stealing some of our pickaxes and shovels.
Thirdly, A *circumbendibus* described by a few
daring French dragoons, who succeeded in
getting into the rear of our engineers' camp,
at that time unguarded, and lightened some
of the officers of their epaulettes. Lastly,
Two field-pieces taken by the enemy to the
opposite side of the river, enfilading one of
our parallels, and materially disturbing the

harmony within, as a cannon-shot is no very welcome guest among gentlemen who happen to be lodged in a straight ditch, without the power of *cutting* it.

Our batteries were supplied with ammunition, by the Portuguese militia, from Elvas, a string of whom used to arrive every day, reaching nearly from the one place to the other (twelve miles), each man carrying a twenty-four pound shot, and cursing all the way and back again.

The Portuguese artillery, under British officers, was uncommonly good. I used to be much amused in looking at a twelve-gun breaching-battery of theirs.

They knew the position of all the enemy's guns which could bear upon them, and had one man posted to watch them, to give notice of what was coming, whether a shot or a shell, who, accordingly, kept calling out, " *bomba, balla, balla, bomba;*" and they ducked their heads until the missile past : but, sometimes he would see a general discharge from all arms,

when he threw himself down, screaming out
" *Jesus, todos, todos!* " meaning " every thing."

An officer of ours was sent one morning,
before day-light, with ten men, to dig holes for
themselves, opposite to one of the enemy's guns,
which had been doing a great deal of mischief
the day before, and he had soon the satisfaction
of knowing the effect of his practice, by seeing
them stopping up the embrasure with sand-
bags. After waiting a little, he saw them beginning to remove the bags, when he made his
men open upon it again, and they were instantly replaced without the guns being fired;
presently he saw the huge cocked hat of a
French officer make its appearance on the rampart, near to the embrasure; but knowing, by
experience, that the *head* was somewhere in the
neighourhood, he watched until the flash of a
musket, through the long grass, showed the
position of the owner, and, calling one of his
best shots, he desired him to take deliberate
aim at the spot, and lent his shoulder as a rest,

to give it more elevation. Bang went the shot, and it was the finishing flash for the Frenchman, for they saw no more of *him*, although his cocked hat maintained its post until dark.

In proportion as the grand crisis approached, the anxiety of the soldiers increased; not on account of any doubt or dread as to the result, but for fear that the place should be surrendered without standing an assault; for, singular as it may appear, although there was a certainty of about one man out of every three being knocked down, there were, perhaps, not three men, in the three divisions, who would not rather have braved all the chances than receive it tamely from the hands of the enemy. So great was the rage for passports into eternity, in our battalion, on that occasion, that even the officers' servants insisted on taking their places in the ranks; and I was obliged to leave my baggage in charge of a man who had been wounded some days before.

On the 6th of April, three practicable breaches

had been effected, and arrangements were made for assaulting the town that night. The third division, by escalade, at the castle; a brigade of the fifth division, by escalade, at the opposite side of the town; while the fourth and light divisions were to storm the breaches. The whole were ordered to be formed for the attack at eight o'clock.

STORMING OF BADAJOS,

April 6th, 1812.

Our division formed for the attack of the left breach in the same order as at Ciudad Rodrigo; the command of it had now devolved upon our commandant, Colonel Barnard. I was then the acting adjutant of four companies, under Colonel Cameron, who were to line the crest of the glacis, and to fire at the ramparts and the top of the left breach.

The enemy seemed aware of our intentions. The fire of artillery and musketry, which, for three weeks before, had been incessant, both from the town and trenches, had now entirely ceased, as if by mutual consent, and a death-like silence, of nearly an hour, preceded the awful scene of carnage.

The signal to advance was made about nine o'clock, and our four companies led the way. Colonel Cameron and myself had reconnoitred the ground so accurately by day-light, that we succeeded in bringing the head of our column to the very spot agreed on, opposite to the left breach, and then formed line to the left, without a word being spoken, each man lying down as he got into line, with the muzzle of his rifle over the edge of the ditch, between the pallisades, all ready to open. It was tolerably clear above, and we distinctly saw *their* heads lining the ramparts; but there was a sort of haze on the ground which, with the colour of our dress, prevented them from seeing us, although only a few yards asunder. One of their sentries, how-ever, challenged us twice, " *qui vive*," and, re-ceiving no reply, he fired off his musket, which was followed by their drums beating to arms; but *we* still remained perfectly quiet, and all was silence again for the space of five or ten minutes, when the head of the forlorn hope at length came up, and we took advantage of the first fire, while the enemy's heads were yet visible.

The scene that ensued furnished as respectable a representation of hell itself as fire, and sword, and human sacrifices could make it; for, in one instant, every engine of destruction was in full operation.

It is in vain to attempt a description of it. We were entirely excluded from the right breach by an inundation which the heavy rains had enabled the enemy to form; and the two others were rendered totally impracticable by their interior defences.

The five succeeding hours were therefore past in the most gallant and hopeless attempts, on the part of individual officers, forming up fifty or a hundred men at a time at the foot of the breach, and endeavouring to carry it by desperate bravery; and, fatal as it proved to each

gallant band, in succession, yet, fast as one dis-
solved, another was formed. We were informed,
about twelve at night, that the third division
had established themselves in the castle; but,
as its situation and construction did not permit
them to extend their operations beyond it at the
moment, it did not in the least affect our opponents at the breach, whose defence continued
as obstinate as ever.

I was near Colonel Barnard after midnight,
when he received repeated messages, from Lord
Wellington, to withdraw from the breach, and
to form the division for a renewal of the attack
at day-light; but, as fresh attempts continued
to be made, and the troops were still pressing
forward into the ditch, it went against his gallant soul to order a retreat while yet a chance
remained; but, after heading repeated attempts
himself, he saw that it was hopeless, and the
order was reluctantly given about two o'clock in
the morning. We fell back about three hundred
yards, and re-formed all that remained to us.

Our regiment, alone, had to lament the loss of

twenty-two officers killed and wounded, ten of
whom were killed, or afterwards died of their
wounds. We had scarcely got our men together
when we were informed of the success of the
fifth division in their escalade, and that the
enemy were, in consequence, abandoning the
breaches, and we were immediately ordered
forward to take possession of them. On our
arrival, we found them entirely evacuated, and
had not occasion to fire another shot; but we
found the utmost difficulty, and even danger, in
getting in in the dark, even without opposition.
As soon as we succeeded in establishing our
battalion inside, we sent piquets into the different streets and lanes leading from the breach,
and kept the remainder in hand until day
should throw some light on our situation.

When I was in the act of posting one of the
piquets, a man of ours brought me a prisoner,
telling me that he was the governor; but the
other immediately said that he had only called
himself so, the better to ensure his protection;
and then added, that he was the colonel of one

of the French regiments, and that all his surviving officers were assembled at his quarters,
in a street close by, and would surrender themselves to any officer who would go with him for that
purpose. I accordingly took two or three men
with me, and, accompanying him there, found fifteen or sixteen of them assembled, and all seeming
very much surprised at the unexpected termi-
nation of the siege. They could not comprehend
under what circumstances the town had been
lost, and repeatedly asked me how I had got in;
but I did not choose to explain further than
simply telling them that I had entered at the
breach, coupling the information with a look
which was calculated to convey somewhat more
than I knew myself; for, in truth, when I began
to recollect that a few minutes before had seen
me retiring from the breach, under a fanciful
overload of degradation, I thought that I had
now as good a right as any man to be astonished
at finding myself *lording* it over the officers of a
French battalion; nor was I much wiser than
they were, as to the manner of its accomplish-

ment. They were all very much dejected, excepting their major, who was a big jolly-looking Dutchman, with medals enough, on his left breast, to have furnished the window of a tolerable toy-shop. His accomplishments were after the manner of Captain Dougal Dalgetty; and, while he cracked his joke, he was not inattentive to the cracking of the corks from the many wine-bottles which his colonel placed on the table successively, along with some cold meat, for general refreshment, prior to marching into captivity, and which I, though a free man, was not too proud to join them in.

When I had allowed their chief a reasonable time to secure what valuables he wished, about his person, he told me that he had two horses in the stable, which, as he would no longer be permitted to keep, he recommended me to take; and, as a horse is the only thing on such occasions that an officer can permit himself to consider a legal prize, I caused one of them to be saddled, and his handsome black mare thereby became my charger during the remainder of the war.

In proceeding with my prisoners towards the breach, I took, by mistake, a different road to that I came; and, as numbers of Frenchmen were lurking about for a safe opportunity of surrendering themselves, about a hundred additional ones added themselves to my column, as we moved along, *jabbering* their native dialect so loudly, as nearly to occasion a dire catastrophe, as it prevented me from hearing some one challenge in my front; but, fortunately, it was repeated, and I instantly answered; for Colonel Barnard and Sir Colin Campbell had a piquet of our men, drawn across the street, on the point of sending a volley into us, thinking that we were a rallied body of the enemy.

The whole of the garrison were marched off, as prisoners, to Elvas, about ten o'clock in the morning, and our men were then permitted to fall out, to enjoy themselves for the remainder of the day, as a reward for having kept together so long as they were wanted. The whole of the three divisions were, by this time, loose in the town ; and the usual frightful scene of plunder commenced, which the officers thought it necessary to avoid for the moment, by retiring to the camp.

We went into the town on the morning of the 8th, to endeavour to collect our men, but only succeeded in part, as the same extraordinary scene of plunder and rioting still continued. Wherever there was any thing to eat or drink, the only saleable commodities, the soldiers had turned the shopkeepers out of doors, and placed themselves regularly behind the counter, selling off the contents of the shop. By and bye, another and a stronger party would kick those out in their turn, and there was no end to the succession of self-elected shopkeepers, until Lord Wellington found that, to restore order, severe measures must be resorted to. On the third day, he caused a Portuguese brigade to be marched in, and kept standing to their arms, in the great square, where the provost-martial erected a gallows, and proceeded to suspend a few of the delinquents, which very quickly cleared the town of the remainder, and enabled us to give a more satisfactory account of our battalion than we had hitherto been able to do.

It is wonderful how such scenes as these will deaden men's finer feelings, and with what apathy it enables them to look upon the sufferings of their fellow creatures! The third day after the fall of the town, I rode, with Colonel Cameron, to take a bathe in the Guadiana, and, in passing the verge of the camp of the 5th division, we saw two soldiers standing at the door of a small shed, or outhouse, shouting, waving their caps, and making signs that they wanted to speak to us. We rode up to see what they wanted, and found that the poor fellows had each lost a leg. They told us that a surgeon had dressed their wounds on the night of the assault, but that they had ever since been without food or assistance of any kind, although they, each day, had opportunities of soliciting the aid of many of their comrades, from whom they could obtain nothing but promises. In short, surrounded by thousands of their countrymen within call, and not more than three hundred yards from their own regiment, they were unable to interest any one in their behalf, and were literally starving.

It is unnecessary to say that we instantly galloped back to the camp and had them removed to the hospital.

On the morning of the 7th, when some of our officers were performing the last duties to their fallen comrades, one of them had collected the bodies of four of our young officers, who had been slain. He was in the act of digging a grave for them, when an officer of the guards, arrived on the spot, from a distant division of the army, and demanded tidings of his brother, who was at that moment lying a naked lifeless corpse, under his very eyes. The officer had the presence of mind to see that the corpse was not recognized, and, wishing to spare the other's feelings, told him that his brother was dangerously wounded, but that he would hear more of him by going out to the camp; and thither the other immediately bent his steps, with a seeming *presentiment* of the sad intelligence that awaited him.

April 9th.—As I had not seen my domestic since· the storming of the town, I concluded that he had been killed; but he turned up this morning, with a tremendous gash on his head, and mounted on the top of a horse nearly twenty feet high, carrying under his arm one of those glass cases which usually stand on the counters of jewellers' shops, filled with all manner of trinkets. He looked exactly like the ghost of a horse pedler.

April 10th.—The devil take the man who stole my donkey last night.

April 11th.—Marched again for the neighbourhood of Ciudad Rodrigo, with the long-accustomed sounds of cannon and musketry ringing in my fanciful ears as merrily as if the instruments themselves were still playing.

Sir Sidney Beckwith, one of the fathers of the rifles, was, at this time, obliged to proceed to England for the recovery of health, and did not again return to the Peninsula. In his depar-

ture, that army lost one of the ablest of its outpost generals. Few officers knew so well how
to make the most of a small force. His courage,
coupled with his thorough knowledge of the soldier's character, was of that cool intrepid kind,
that would, at any time, convert a routed rabble
into an orderly effective force. A better officer,
probably, never led a brigade into the field !

CHAP X.

A Farewell Address to Portalegré. History of a Night in Castello Branco. Regimental Colours lost, with Directions where to find them. Cases in which a Victory is sometimes won by those who lost it. Advance to Salamanca. The City. The British Position on St. Christoval. Affair in Position. Marmont's Change of Position and Retreat. A Case of Bad Luck. Advance to Rueda, and Customs there. Retire to Castrejon. Affairs on the 18th and 19th of July. Battle of Salamanca, and Defeat of the Enemy.

April 13th, 1812.—Quartered at Portalegré.

Dear Portalegré!

I cannot quit thee, for the fourth and last time, without a parting tribute to the remembrance of thy wild romantic scenery, and to the kindness and hospitality of thy worthy citizens! May thy gates continue shut to thine enemies as heretofore, and, as heretofore, may they ever prove those of happiness to thy friends! Dear nuns of Santa Clara! I thank thee for the enjoyment of many an hour of nothingness; and thine, Santa Barbara, for many of a more intellectual cast! May the voice of thy chapel-organ continue unrivalled but by the voices of thy lovely choristers! and may the piano in thy refectory be replaced by a better, in which the harmony of strings may supersede the clattering of ivories! May the sweets which thou hast lavished on us be showered upon thee ten thousand fold! And may those accursed iron bars divide thee as effectually from death as they did from us!!!

April 15th.—Quartered at Castello Branco.

This town had been so often visited by the French and us, alternately, that the inhabitants, at length, confounded their friends with their foes; and by treating both sides as enemies, they succeeded in making them so.

When I went this evening to present my billet

on a respectable looking house, the door was opened by the lady of it, wearing a most gingerly aspect. She told me, with an equivocal sort of look, that she had two spare beds in the house, and that either of them were at my service; and, by way of illustration, shewed me into a sort of servant's room, off the kitchen, half full of apples, onions, potatoes, and various kinds of lumber, with a dirty looking bed in one corner; and, on my requesting to see the other, she conducted me up to the garret, into the very counterpart of the one below, though the room was somewhat differently garnished. I told her, that they were certainly two capital beds; but, as I was a modest person, and disliked all extremes, that I should be quite satisfied with any one on the floor which I had not yet seen. This, however, she told me, was impossible, as every one of them were required by her own family. While we were descending the stair, disputing the point, I caught the handle of the first door that I came to, twisted it open, and seeing it a neat little room, with

H

nothing but a table and two or three chairs, I told her that it would suit me perfectly; and, desiring her to have a good mattress with clean linen, laid in one corner of it, by nine o'clock; adding a few hints, to satisfy her that I was quite in earnest, I went to dine with my messmates.

When I returned to the house, about ten o'clock, I was told that I should find a light in the room and my bed ready. I accordingly ascended, and found every thing as represented; and, in addition thereto, I found another bed lying alongside of mine, containing a huge fat friar, with a bald pate, fast asleep, and blowing the most tremendous nasal trumpet that I ever heard! As my *friend* had evidently been placed there for my annoyance, I did not think it necessary to use much ceremony in getting rid of him; and, catching him by the two ears, I raised him up on his legs, while he groaned in a seeming agonized doubt, whether the pain was inflicted by a man or a nightmare; and before he had time to get himself broad awake, I had chucked

him and his clothing, bed and bedding, out at
the door, which I locked, and enjoyed a sound
sleep the remainder of the night.

They offered me no further molestation; but,
in taking my departure, at daylight, next morning, I observed my landlady reconnoitring me
from an up-stairs window, and thought it prudent not to go too near it.

While we had been employed at Badajos,
Marmont had advanced in the north, and
blockaded Ciudad Rodrigo and Almeida, sending advanced parties into the frontier towns of
Portugal, to the confusion and consternation of
the Portuguese militia, who had been stationed
for their protection; and who, quite satisfied
with the *report* of their coming, did not think it
necessary to wait the report of their cannon.
Marshal Beresford, in his paternal address to
" *Los Valerossos*," in commemoration of their
conduct on this occasion, directed that the colours of each regiment should be lodged in the
town-halls of their respective districts, until they
each provided themselves with *a pair* out of the

ranks of the enemy; but I never heard that any
of them were redeemed in the manner prescribed.

The French retired upon Salamanca on our
approach; and we resumed our former quarters without opposition.

Hitherto we had been fighting the description
of battle in which John Bull glories so much—
gaining a brilliant and useless victory against
great odds. But we were now about to contend
for fame on equal terms; and, having tried both,
I will say, without partiality, that I would rather
fight one man than two any day; for I have
never been quite satisfied that the additional
quantum of glory altogether compensated for
the proportionate loss of substance; a victory
of that kind being a doubtful and most unsatis-
factory one to the performers, with each occupying the same ground *after*, that they did
before; and the whole merit resting with the
side which did not happen to begin it.

We remained about two months in cantonments, to recover the effects of the late sieges;
and as by that time all the perforated skins and

repairable cracked limbs had been mended, the army was assembled in front of Ciudad Rodrigo, to commence what may be termed the second campaign of 1812.

The enemy retired from Salamanca on our approach, leaving garrisons in three formidable little forts, which they had erected on the most commanding points of the city, and which were immediately invested by a British division.

Salamanca, as a city, appeared to me to be more ancient than respectable ; for, excepting an old cathedral and a new square, I saw nothing in it worth looking at, always saving and excepting their pretty little girls, who (the deuce take them) cost me two nights good sleep. For, by way of *doing a little dandy* in passing through such a celebrated city, I disencumbered the under part of my saddle of the blanket, and the upper part of the boat-cloak with which it was usually adorned ; and the penalty which I paid for my gentility was, sleeping the next two nights in position two miles in front of the town, while these useful appendages were lying on the baggage two miles in rear of it.

The heights of St. Christoval, which we occupied as a position to cover the siege, were strong, but quite unsheltered, and unfurnished with either wood or water. We were indebted for our supplies of the latter to the citizens of Salamanca; while stubbles and dry grass were our only fuel.

Marmont came down upon us the first night with a thundering cannonade, and placed his army *en masse* on the plain before us, almost within gun shot. I was told that, while Lord Wellington was riding along the line, under a fire of artillery, and accompanied by a numerous staff, that a brace of greyhounds, in pursuit of a hare, passed close to him. He was, at the moment, in earnest conversation with General Castanos; but the instant he observed them, he gave the view hallo, and went after them at full speed, to the utter astonishment of his foreign accompaniments. Nor did he stop until he saw the hare killed; when he returned, and resumed the commander-in-chief, as if nothing had occurred.

The enemy, next morning, commenced a sharp attack on our advanced post, in the village of Moresco; and, as it continued to be fed by both sides, there was every appearance of its bringing on a general action; but they desisted towards the afternoon, and the village remained divided between us.

Marmont, after looking at us for several days, did not think it prudent to risk an attack on our present post; and, as the telegraph-rockets from the town told him that his garrison was reduced to extremity, he crossed the Tormes, on the night of the 26th June, in the hopes of being able to relieve them from that side of the river. Our division followed his movement, and took post, for the night, at Aldea Lingua. They sent forward a strong reconnoitring party at daylight next morning, but they were opposed by General Bock's brigade of heavy German dragoons, who would not permit them to see more than was necessary ; and, as the forts fell into our hands the same night, Marmont had no longer an object in remaining there, and fell back, behind the Douro, occupying the line of Toro and Torodesillas.

By the accidental discharge of a musket, one day last year, the ramrod entered the belly, passed through the body, and the end of it stuck in the back-bone of one of the soldiers of our division, from whence it was actually hammered out with a stone. The poor fellow recovered, and joined his regiment, as well as ever he had been, and was, last night, unfortunately drowned, while bathing in the Tormes.

When the enemy retired, our division advanced and occupied Rueda, a handsome little town, on the left bank of the Douro.

It abounded in excellent wines, and our usual evening dances began there to be graced by a superior class of females to what they had hitherto been accustomed. I remember that, in passing the house of the sexton, one evening, I saw his daughter baking a loaf of bread; and, falling

desperately in love with both her and the loaf, I
carried the one to the ball and the other to my
quarters. A woman was a woman in those days;
and every officer made it a point of duty to marshal as many as he could to the general assembly,
no matter whether they were countesses or *sex-*
tonesses; and although we, in consequence, frequently incurred the most indelible disgrace among
the better orders of our indiscriminate collection, some of whom would retire in disgust; yet,
as a sufficient number generally remained for
our evening's amusement, and we were only
birds of passage, it was a matter of the most
perfect indifference to us what they thought;
we followed the same course wherever we
went.

The French army having, in the mean time,
been largely reinforced; and, as they commanded
the passage of the Douro, we were in hourly
expectation of an offensive movement from
them. As a precautionary measure, one-half of
our division bivouacked, every night, in front
of the town. On the evening of the 16th of

July, it was our turn to be in quarters, and we were in the full enjoyment of our usual evening's amusement, when the bugles sounded to arms.

As we had previously experienced two false alarms in the same quarters, we thought it more than probable that this might prove one also; and, therefore, prevailed upon the ladies to enjoy themselves, until our return, upon the good things which we had provided for their refreshment, and out of which I hope they drew enough of consolation for our absence, as we have not seen them since.

After forming on our alarm-post, we were moved off, in the dark, we knew not whither; but every man following the one before him, with the most implicit confidence, until, after marching all night, we found ourselves, on the following morning, at daylight, near the village of Castrejon, where we bivouacked for the day.

I was sent on piquet on the evening of the 19th, to watch a portion of the plain before us; and, soon after sunrise on the following morning, a cannonade commenced, behind a hill, to my

right; and, though the combatants were not
visible, it was evident that they were not dealing
in blank-cartridge, as mine happened to be the
pitching-post of all the enemy's round shot.
While I was attentively watching its progress,
there arose, all at once, behind the rising ground
to my left, a yell of the most terrific import;
and convinced that it would give instantaneous
birth to as hideous a body, it made me look,
with an eye of lightning, at the ground around
me; and, seeing a broad deep ditch within a
hundred yards, I lost not a moment in placing it
between my piquet and the extraordinary sound.
I had scarcely effected the movement, when
Lord Wellington, with his staff, and a cloud of
French and English dragoons and horse artillery
intermixed, came over the hill at full cry, and
all hammering at each others' heads in one confused mass, over the very ground I had that
instant quitted. It appeared that his Lordship
had gone there to reconnoitre, covered by two
guns and two squadrons of cavalry, who, by
some accident, were surprised, and charged by

a superior body of the enemy, and sent tumbling in upon us in the manner described. A piquet of the forty-third had formed on our right, and we were obliged to remain passive spectators of such an extraordinary scene going on within a few yards of us, as we could not fire without an equal chance of shooting some of our own side. Lord Wellington and his staff, with the two guns, took shelter, for the moment, behind us, while the cavalry went sweeping along our front, where, I suppose, they picked up some rein-forcement, for they returned, almost instantly, in the same confused mass; but the French were now the flyers; and, I must do them the justice to say, that they got off in a manner highly creditable to themselves. I saw one, in particular, defending himself against two of ours; and he would have made his escape from both, but an officer of our dragoons came down the hill, and took him in flank, at full speed, sending man and horse rolling, headlong, on the plain.

I was highly interested, all this time, in observing the distinguished characters which this unlooked-for *turn-up* had assembled around us. Marshal Beresford and the greater part of the staff remained with their swords drawn, and the Duke himself did not look more than half-pleased, while he silently despatched some of them with orders. General Alten, and his huge German orderly dragoon, with their swords drawn, cursed, the whole time, to a very large amount ; but, as it was in German, I had not the full benefit of it. He had an opposition swearer in Captain Jenkinson, of the artillery, who commanded the two guns, and whose oaths were chiefly aimed at himself for his folly, as far as I could understand, in putting so much con-fidence in his covering party, that he had not thought it necessary to unfix the catch which horse-artillerymen, I believe, had to prevent their swords quitting the scabbards when they are not wanted, and which, on this occasion, prevented their jumping forth when they were so unexpectedly called for.

The straggling enemy had scarcely cleared

away from our front, when Lord Combermere came, from the right, with a reinforcement of cavalry; and our piquet was, at the same moment, ordered to join the battalion.

The movements which followed presented the most beautiful military spectacle imaginable. The enemy were endeavouring to turn our left; and, in making a counteracting movement, the two armies were marching in parallel lines, close to each other, on a perfect plain, each ready to take advantage of any opening of the other, and exchanging round shot as they moved along. Our division brought up the rear of the infantry, marching with the order and precision of a field-day, in open column of companies, and in perfect readiness to receive the enemy in any shape; who, on their part, had a huge cavalry force close at hand, and equally ready to pounce upon us. Our movement was supported by a formidable body of our own dragoons; and, as we drew near the bank of the small river Guerrena, our horse-artillery continued to file in the same line, to attract the attention of the enemy, while we gradually distanced them a little, and crossed the river into a position on the high grounds beyond it. The enemy passed the river, on our left, and endeavoured to force that part of the position; but the troops who were stationed there drove them back, with great loss; and at dark the firing ceased.

During the early part of the 19th there appeared to be no movements on either side; but, in the afternoon, having fallen asleep in my tent, I was awoke by the whistling of a cannon shot; and was just beginning to abuse my servant for not having called me sooner, when we were ordered to stand to our arms; and, as the enemy were making a movement to our right, we made a corresponding one. The cannonade did not cease until dark, when we lay down by our arms, the two armies very near to each other, and fully expecting a general action on the morrow.

July 20th.—We stood to our arms an hour before daylight, and Lord Wellington held out every inducement for his opponent to attack him; but Marmont evaded it, and continued his movement on our right, which obliged us to continue ours, towards Salamanca; and we were a great part of this day in parallel lines with them, the same as on the 18th.

July 21st.—We crossed the Tormes just before dark this evening, about two miles above Salamanca, the enemy having passed it higher up. Before reaching our ground, we experienced one of the most tremendous thunderstorms that I ever witnessed. A sheet of lightning struck the head of our column, where I happened to be riding, and deprived me of the use of my optics for at least ten minutes. A great many of our dragoon horses broke from their piqueting during the storm, and galloped past us into the French lines. We lay by our arms on the banks of the river, and it continued to rain in torrents the whole of the night.

BATTLE OF SALAMANCA.

July 22d.—A sharp fire of musketry commenced at day light in the morning; but, as it did not immediately concern us, and was nothing unusual, we took no notice of it; but busied ourselves in getting our arms and our bodies disengaged from the rust and the wet, engendered by the storm of the past night.

About ten o'clock, our division was ordered to stand to their arms, and then moved into position, with our left resting on the Tormes, and our right extending along a ridge of rising ground, thinly interspered with trees, beyond which the other divisions were formed in continuation, with the exception of the third, which still remained on the opposite bank of the river.

The enemy were to be seen in motion on the opposite ridges, and a straggling fire of musketry, with an occasional gun, acted as a sort of prelude to the approaching conflict. We heard,

about this time, that Marmont had just sent to
his *ci-devant* landlord, in Salamanca, to desire
that he would have the usual dinner ready for
himself and staff at six o'clock; and so satisfied
was " mine host" of the infallibility of the
French Marshal, that he absolutely set about
making the necessary preparations.

There assuredly never was an army so anxious
as ours was to be brought into action on this
occasion. They were a magnificent body of
well-tried soldiers, highly equipped, and in the
highest health and spirits, with the most devoted
confidence in their leader, and an invincible confidence in themselves. The retreat of the four
preceding days had annoyed us beyond measure,
for we believed that we were nearly equal to the
enemy in point of numbers; and the idea of our
retiring before an equal number of any troops in
the world was not to be endured with common
patience.

We were kept the whole of the forenoon in
the most torturing state of suspense through
contradictory reports. One passing officer tel-

ling us that he had just heard the order given to attack, and the next asserting, with equal confidence, that he had just heard the order to retreat; and it was not until about two o'clock in the afternoon, that affairs began to wear a more decided aspect; and when our own eyes and ears at length conveyed the wished-for tidings that a battle was inevitable; for we saw the enemy beginning to close upon our right, and the cannonade had become general along the whole line. Lord Wellington, about the same time, ordered the movement which decided the fate of the day—that of bringing the third division, from beyond the river on our left, rapidly to our extreme right, turning the enemy, in their attempt to turn us, and commencing the offensive with the whole of his right wing. The effect was instantaneous and decisive, for although some obstinate and desperate fighting took place in the centre, with various success, yet the victory was never for a moment in doubt; and the enemy were soon in full retreat, leaving seven thousand prisoners, two eagles, and eleven pieces of artillery in our hands. Had we been favoured with two hours more daylight, their loss would have been incalculable, for they committed a blunder at starting, which they never got time to retrieve; and, their retreat was, therefore, commenced in such disorder, and with a river in their rear, that nothing but darkness could have saved them.

CHAP. XI.

Distinguished Characters. A Charge of Dragoons. A Charge against the Nature of Things. Olmeda and the French General, Ferez. Advance towards Madrid. Adventures of my Dinner. The Town of Segovia. El Palacio del Rio Frio. The Escurial. Enter Madrid. Rejoicings. Nearly happy. Change of a Horse. Change of Quarters. A Change confounded. Retire towards Salamanca. Boar-Hunt, Dinner-Hunt, and Bull-Hunt. A Portuguese Funeral conducted by Rifle Undertakers.

THE third division, under Sir Edward Pakenham, the artillery, and some regiments of dragoons, particularly distinguished themselves. But our division, very much to our annoyance, came in for a very slender portion of this day's glory. We were exposed to a cannonade the whole of the afternoon ; but, as we were not permitted to advance until very late, we had only an opportunity of throwing a few straggling shot at the fugitives, before we lost sight of them in the dark; and then bivouacked for the night near the village of Huerta, (I think it was called).

We started after them at daylight next morning; and, crossing at a ford of the Tormes, we found their rear-guard, consisting of three regiments of infantry, with some cavalry and artillery, posted on a formidable height above the village of Serna. General Bock, with his brigade of heavy German dragoons, immediately went at them; and, putting their cavalry to flight, he broke through their infantry, and took or destroyed the whole of them. This was one of the most gallant charges recorded in history. I saw many of these fine fellows lying dead along with their horses, on which they were still astride, with the sword firmly grasped in the hand, as they had fought the instant before; and several of them still wearing a look of fierce defiance, which death itself had been unable to quench.

We halted for the night at a village near Penaranda. I took possession of the church; and finding the floor strewed with the paraphernalia of priesthood, I selected some silk gowns, and other gorgeous trappings, with which I made a bed for myself in the porch, and where, " if all had been gold that glittered," I should have looked a jewel indeed ; but it is lamentable to think, that, among the multifarious blessings we enjoy in this life, we should never be able to get a dish of glory and a dish of beefsteak on the same day; in consequence of which, the heart, which ought properly to be soaring in the clouds, or, at all events, in a castle half way up, is more generally to be found grovelling about a hen-roost, in the vain hope, that, if it cannot get hold of the hen herself, it may at least hit upon an egg; and such, I remember, was the state of my feelings on this occasion, in consequence of my having dined the three preceding days on the half of my inclinations.

We halted the next night in the handsome little town of Olmeda, which had just been evacuated by the enemy. The French General, Ferez, died there, in consequence of the wounds which he received at the battle of Salamanca, and his remains had, the night before, been consigned to the earth, with the highest honours, and a canopy of laurel placed over his grave : but the French had no sooner left the town, than the inhabitants exhumed the body, cut off the head, and spurned it with the greatest indignity. They were in hopes that this line of conduct would have proved a passport to our affections, and conducted us to the spot, as to a trophy that they were proud of; but we expressed the most unfeigned horror and indignation at their proceeding; and, getting some soldiers to assist us, we carefully and respectfully replaced his remains in the grave. His *was* a noble head ; and even in death, it looked the brave, the gallant soldier. Our conduct had such an effect on the Spaniards, that they brought back the canopy, of their own accord, and promised, solemnly, that the grave should, henceforth, rest undisturbed.

July 26th.—We arrived on the banks of

the Douro, within a league of Valladolid, where we halted two days; and Lord Wellington, detaching a division of infantry and some cavalry to watch the movements of the defeated army, proceeded with the remainder of us towards Madrid.

August 1st.—On approaching near to our bivouac this afternoon, I saw a good large farmhouse, about a mile off the road; and, getting permission from my commandant, I made a cast thereto, in search of something for dinner. There were two women belonging to the German Legion, smoking their pipes in the kitchen, when I arrived; and, having the highest respect for their marauding qualifications, I began to fear that nothing was to be had, as they were sitting there so quietly. I succeeded, however, in purchasing two pair of chickens; and, neglecting the precaution of unscrewing their necks, I grasped a handful of their legs, and, mounting my horse, proceeded towards the camp; but I had scarcely gone a couple of hundred yards, when they began opening their throats and flapping with their wings, which startled my horse and sent him off at full speed. I lost the rein on one side, and, in attempting to pull him up with the other, I brought his foot into a rut, and down he came, sending me head-foremost into a wet ditch! When I got on my legs, and shook myself a little, I saw each particular hen galloping across the field, screeching with all its might, while the horse was off in a different direction; and, casting a rueful look at the chickens, I naturally followed him, as the most valuable of the collection. Fortunately, a heavy boat-cloak caused the saddle to roll under his belly; and finding that he could not make way in consequence, he quietly waited for me about a quarter of a mile off. When I had re-mounted, I looked back to the scene of my disaster, and saw my two German *friends* busily employed in catching the chickens. I rode towards them, and they were, no doubt, in hopes that I had broken my neck, that they might have the sacking of me, also; for, as I approached, I observed them concealing the fowls under their clothes, while the one took up a position behind the other. After reconnoitring them a short time, I rode up and demanded the fowls, when the one looked at the other, and, in well-feigned astonishment, asked, in *Dutch*, what I could possibly mean? then gave me to understand that they could not comprehend English; but I immediately said, " Come, come ! none of your gammon; you have got my fowls, here's half a dollar for your trouble in catching them, so hand them out." " Oh !" said one of them, in English, " it is de fowl you want," and they then produced them. After paying them the stipulated sum, I wished them all the compliments of the season, and thought myself fortunate in getting off so well; for they were each six feet high, and as strong as a horse, and I felt convinced that they had often thrashed a better man than myself in the course of their military career.

August 7th.—Halted near the ancient town of Segovia, which bears a strong resemblance to the old town of Edinburgh, built on a lofty ridge, that terminates in an abrupt summit, on which stands the fortified tower, celebrated in the Adventures of Gil Blas. It is a fine old town, boasts of a superb Roman aqueduct, and is famous for ladies' shoes.

Our bivouac, this evening, was on the banks of El Rio Frio, near to a new hunting-palace of the King of Spain. It was a large quadrangular building, each side full of empty rooms, with nothing but their youth to recommend them.

On the 9th, we crossed the Guadarama mountains, and halted, for the night, in the park of the Escurial.

I had, from childhood upwards, considered this palace as the eighth wonder of the world, and was, therefore, proportionately disappointed at finding it a huge, gloomy, unmeaning pile of building, looking somewhat less interesting than the wild craggy mountain opposite, and without containing a single room large enough to flog a cat in. The only apartment that I saw worth looking at was the one in which their *dead kings live!*

ENTERED MADRID,

August 13th, 1812.

As we approached the capital, imagination was busy in speculating on the probable nature of our reception. The peasantry, with whom we had hitherto been chiefly associated, had imbibed a rooted hatred to the French, caused by the wanton cruelties experienced at their hands, both in their persons and their property; otherwise they were a cheerful, hospitable, and orderly people, and, had they been permitted to live in peace and quietness, it was a matter of the most perfect indifference to them whether Joseph, Ferdinand, or the ghost of Don Quixotte was their king. But the citizens of Madrid had been living four years in comparative peace, under the dominion of a French government,

and in the enjoyment of all the gaieties of that
luxurious court; to which, if I add that we entertained, at that time, some slight jealousy
regarding the pretensions of the French officers
to the favours of the fair, I believe the pre-
vailing opinion was that *we* should be considered
as the intruders. It was, therefore, a matter
of the most unexpected exultation, when we
entered it, on the afternoon of the 13th of August,
to find ourselves hailed as liberators, with the
most joyous acclamations, by surrounding mul-
titudes, who continued their rejoicings for three
successive days. By day, the riches of each
house were employed in decorations to its ex-
terior; and, by night, they were brilliantly illuminated, during which time all business was
suspended, and the whole population of the
city crowded the streets, emulating each other
in heaping honours and caresses upon us.

King Joseph had retired on our approach,
leaving a garrison in the fortified palace of El
Retiro; but they surrendered some days afterwards, and we remained there for three months,

basking in the sunshine of beauty, harmony, and peace. I shall ever look back to that period as the most pleasing event of my military life.

The only bar to our perfect felicity was the want of money, as, independent of long arrears, already due, the military chest continued so very poor that it could not afford to give us more than a fortnight's pay during these three months; and, as nobody could, would, or should give cash for bills, we were obliged to sell silver spoons, watches, and every thing of value that we stood possessed of, to purchase the common necessaries of life.

My Irish *criado*, who used to take uncommon liberties with my property, having been two or three days in the rear, with the baggage, at the time of the battle of Salamanca, took upon himself to exchange my baggage-horse for another; and his apology for so doing was, that the one he had got was twice as big as the one he gave! The additional size, however, so far from being an advantage, proved quite the reverse; for I found that he could eat as much as he could carry, and, as he was obliged to carry all that he had to eat, I was forced to put him on half allowance, to make room for my baggage; in consequence of which, every bone in his body soon became so *pointed* that I could easily have hung my hat on any part of his hind quarters. I therefore took advantage of our present repose to let him have the benefit of a full allowance, that enabled me to effect an exchange between him and a mule, getting five dollars to the bargain, which made me one of the happiest and, I believe, also, one of the richest men in the army. I expended the first dollar next day, in getting admission to a bullfight, in their national amphitheatre, where the first thing that met my astonished eyes was a mad bull giving the finishing *prode* to my unfortunate big horse.

Lord Wellington, with some divisions of the army, proceeded, about the beginning of September, to undertake the siege of Burgos, leaving those at Madrid, under the orders of Sir Rowland Hill, so that, towards the end of October, our delightful sojourn there drew perceptibly to a close, for it was known that King Joseph, with the forces under Soult and Jourdan, now united, were moving upon Aranjuez, and that all, excepting our own division, were already in motion, to dispute the passage of the Tagus, and to cover the capital. About four o'clock on the morning of the 23d of October, we received orders to be on our alarm-posts at six, and, as soon as we had formed, we were marched to the city of Alcala.

October 27th.—We were all this day marching to Arganda, and all night marching back again. If any one thing is more particularly damned than another it is a march of this kind.

October 30th.—An order arrived, from Lord Wellington, for our corps of the army to fall back upon Salamanca ; we, therefore, returned to Madrid, and, after halting outside the gates until we were joined by Skerret's division, from Cadiz, we bade a last sorrowful adieu to our friends in the city, and commenced our retreat.

October 31st.—Halted for the night in the park of the Escurial. It is amusing, on a division's first taking up its ground, to see the numbers of hares that are, every instant, starting up among the men, and the scrambling and shouting of the soldiers for the prize. This day, when the usual shout was given, every man ran, with his cap in his hand, to endeavour to capture poor *puss*, as he imagined, but which turned out to be two wild boars, who contrived to make room for themselves so long as there was nothing but men's caps to contend with; but they very soon had as many bayonets as bristles in their backs. We re-crosed the Guadarama mountains next morning.

November 2d.—Halted, this night, in front of a small town, the name of which I do not recollect. It was beginning to get dark by the time I had posted our guards and piquets, when I rode into it, to endeavour to find my messmates, who, I knew, had got a dinner waiting for me somewhere.

I entered a large square, or market-place,

and found it crowded with soldiers of all nations, most of them three-parts drunk, and in the midst of whom a mad bull was performing the most extraordinary feats, quite unnoticed, excepting by those who had the misfortune to attract his attention. The first intimation that I had of him was his charging past me, and making a thrust at our quarter-master, carrying off a portion of his regimental trousers. He next got a fair toss at a Portuguese soldier, and sent him spinning three or four turns up in the air. I was highly amused in observing the fellow's astonishment when he alighted, to see that he had not the remotest idea to what accident he was indebted for such an evolution, although he seemed fully prepared to quarrel with any one who chose to acknowledge any participation in the deed; but the cause of it was, all the time, finding fresh customers, and, making the grand tour of the square with such velocity, I began to fear that I should soon be on his list also, if I did not take shelter in the nearest house, a measure no sooner thought

of than executed. I, therefore, opened a door,
and drove my horse in before me; but there
instantly arose such an uproar within, that I
began to wish myself once more on the outside
on any terms, for it happened to be occupied
by English, Portuguese, and German bul-
lock-drivers, who had been seated round a
table, scrambling for a dinner, when my horse
upset the table, lights, and every thing on
it. The only thing that I could make out amid
their confused curses was, that they had come
to the determination of putting the cause of the
row to death; but, as I begged to differ with
them on that point, I took the liberty of knocking one or two of them down, and finally succeeded in extricating my horse, with whom I
retraced my way to the camp, weary, angry,
and hungry. On my arrival there, I found
an orderly waiting to show me the way to dinner,
which once more restored me to good humour
with myself and all the world; while the adventure afforded my companions a hearty laugh, at
my expense.

November 6th.—In the course of this day's march, while our battalion formed the rearguard, at a considerable distance in the rear of the column, we found a Portuguese soldier, who had been left by his regiment, lying in the middle of the road, apparently dead; but, on examining him more closely, we had reason to think that he was merely in a state of stupor, arising from fatigue and the heat of the weather,— an opinion which caused us no little uneasiness. Although we did not think it quite fair to bury a living man, yet we had no means whatever of carrying him off; and to leave him where he was, would, in all probability, have cost us a number of better lives than his had ever been, for the French, who were then in sight, had hitherto been following us at a very respectable distance; and, had they found that we were retiring in such a hurry as to leave our half-dead people on the road, they would not have been Frenchmen if they did not give us an extra push, to help us along. Under all the circumstances of the case, therefore, although our doctor was of opinion that, with time and attention, he might recover, and not having either the one or the other to spare, the remainder of us, who had voted ourselves into a sort of board of survey, thought it most prudent to find him dead ; and, carrying him a little off the road to the edge of a ravine, we scraped a hole in the sand with our swords, and placed him in it. We covered him but very lightly, and left his head and arms at perfect liberty ; so that, although he might be said to have had both feet in the grave, yet he might still have scrambled out of it, if he could.

CHAP. XII.

Reach Salamanca. Retreat from it. Pig Hunting, an Enemy to Sleep-Hunting. Putting one's Foot in it. Affair on the 17th of November. Bad Legs sometimes last longer than good ones. A Wet Birth. Prospectus of a Day's Work. A lost *déjûné* better than a found one. Advantages not taken. A disagreeable Amusement. End of the Campaign of 1812. Winter Quarters. Orders and Disorders treated. Farewell Opinion of Ancient Allies. My House.

November 7th.—HALTED this night at Alba de Tormes, and next day marched into quarters in Salamanca, where we rejoined Lord Wellington with the army from Burgos.

On the 14th, the British army concentrated on the field of their former glory, in consequence of a part of the French army having effected the passage of the river, above Alba de Tormes. On the 15th, the whole of the enemy's force having passed the river, a cannonade commenced early in the day; and it was the general belief that, ere night, a second battle of Salamanca would be recorded. But, as all the French armies in Spain were now united in our front, and out-numbered us so far, Lord Wellington, seeing no decided advantage to be gained by risking a battle, at length ordered a retreat, which we commenced about three in the afternoon. Our division halted for the night at the entrance of a forest about four miles from Salamanca.

The heavy rains which usually precede the Spanish winter had set in the day before; and, as the roads in that part of the country cease to be roads for the remainder of the season, we were now walking nearly knee deep, in a stiff mud, into which no man could thrust his foot, with the certainty of having a shoe at the end of it when he pulled it out again; and, that we might not be miserable by halves, we had, this evening, to regale our chops with the last morsel of biscuit that they were destined to grind during the retreat.

We cut some boughs of trees to keep us out of the mud, and lay down to sleep on them, wet to the skin; but the cannonade of the afternoon had been succeeded, after dark, by a continued firing of musketry, which led us to believe that our piqûets were attacked, and, in momentary expectation of an order to stand to our arms, we kept ourselves awake the whole night, and were not a little provoked when we found, next morning, that it had been occasioned by numerous stragglers from the different regiments, shooting at the pigs belonging to the peasantry, which were grazing in the wood.

November 16th. — Retiring from daylight until dark through the same description of roads. The French dragoons kept close behind, but did not attempt to molest us. It still continued to rain hard, and we again passed the night in a wood. I was very industriously employed, during the early part of it, feeling, in the dark, for acorns, as a substitute for bread.

November 17th.—At daylight this morning the enemy's cavalry advanced in force; but they were kept in check by the skirmishers of the 14th light dragoons, until the road became open, when we continued our retreat. Our brigade-major was at this time obliged to go to the rear, sick, and I was appointed to act for him.

We were much surprised, in the course of the forenoon, to hear a sharp firing commence behind us, on the very road by which we were retiring; and it was not until we reached the spot that we learnt that the troops who were retreating, by a road parallel to ours, had left it too soon, and enabled some French dragoons, under cover of the forest, to advance unperceived to the flank of our line of march, who, seeing an interval between two divisions of infantry, which was filled with light baggage and some passing officers, dashed at it, and made some prisoners in the scramble of the moment, amongst whom was Lieutenant-General Sir Edward Paget.

Our division formed on the heights above Samunoz to cover the passage of the rivulet, which was so swollen with the heavy rains, as only to be passable at particular fords. While we waited there for the passage of the rest of the army, the enemy, under cover of the forest, was, at the same time, assembling in force close around us; and the moment that we began to descend the hill, towards the rivulet, we were assailed by a heavy fire of cannon and musketry, while their powerful cavalry were in readiness to take advantage of any confusion which might have occurred. We effected the passage, however, in excellent order, and formed on the opposite bank of the stream, where we continued under a cannonade and engaged in a sharp skirmish until dark.

Our loss on this occasion was considerable, but it would have been much greater, had not the enemy's shells buried themselves so deep in the soft ground, that their explosions did little injury. It appeared singular to us, who were not medical men, that an officer and several of our division, who were badly wounded on this occasion, in the leg, and who were sent to the rear on gun-carriages, should have died of a mortification in the limb which was *not* wounded.

When the firing ceased, we received the usual order " to make ourselves comfortable for the night," and I never remember an instance in which we had so much difficulty in obeying it; for the ground we occupied was a perfect flat, which was flooded more than ankle deep with water, excepting here and there, where the higher ground around the roots of trees, presented circles of a few feet of visible earth, upon which we grouped ourselves. Some few fires were kindled, at which we roasted some bits of raw beef on the points of our swords, and eat them by way of a dinner. There was plenty of water to apologize for the want of better fluids, but bread sent no apology at all.

Some divisions of the army had commenced retiring as soon as it was dark, and the whole had been ordered to move, so that the roads might be clear for us before daylight. I was sent twice in the course of the night to see what progress they had made; but such was the state of the roads, that even within an hour of daylight, two divisions, besides our own, were still unmoved, which would consequently delay us so long, that we looked forward to a severe harassing day's fighting; a kind of fighting, too, that is the least palatable of any, where much might be lost, and nothing was to be gained. With such prospects before us, it made my very heart rejoice to see my brigadier's servant commence boiling some chocolate and frying a beef-steak. I watched its progress with a keenness which intense hunger alone could inspire, and was on the very point of having my desires consummated, when the general, getting uneasy at not having received any communication relative to the movements of the morning, and, without considering how feelingly my

stomach yearned for a better acquaintance with
the contents of his frying-pan, desired me to
ride to General Alten for orders. I found the
general at a neighbouring tree; but he cut off
all hopes of my timely return, by desiring me
to remain with him until he received the report
of an officer whom he had sent to ascertain the
progress of the other divisions.

While I was toasting myself at his fire, so
sharply set that I could have eaten one of my
boots, I observed his German orderly dragoon,
at an adjoining fire, stirring up the contents of
a camp-kettle, that once more revived my de-
parting hopes, and I presently had the satisfaction of seeing him dipping in some basins,
presenting one to the general, one to the aide-
de-camp, and a third to myself. The mess
which it contained I found, after swallowing the
whole at a draught, was neither more nor less
than the produce of a piece of beef boiled in
plain water; and, though it would have been
enough to have physicked a dromedary at any
other time, yet, as I could then have made a

good hole in the dromedary himself, it sufficiently satisfied my cravings to make me equal to any thing for the remainder of the day.

We were soon after ordered to stand to our arms, and, as day lit up, a thick haze hung on the opposite hills, which prevented our seeing the enemy; and, as they did not attempt to feel for us, we, contrary to our expectations, commenced our retreat unmolested; nor could we quite believe our good fortune when, towards the afternoon, we had passed several places where they could have assailed us, in flank, with great advantage, and caused us a severe loss, almost in spite of fate; but it afterwards appeared that they were quite knocked up with their exertions in overtaking us the day before, and were unable to follow further. We halted on a swampy height, behind St. Espiritu, and experienced another night of starvation and rain.

I now felt considerably more for my horse than myself, as he had been three days and nights without a morsel of any kind to eat. Our baggage-animals, too, we knew were equally ill off, and, as they always preceded us a day's march, it was highly amusing, whenever we found a dead horse, or a mule, lying on the road-side, to see the anxiety with which every officer went up to reconnoitre him, each fearing that he should have the misfortune to recognize it as his own.

On the 19th of November we arrived at the convent of Caridad, near Ciudad Rodrigo, and once more experienced the comforts of our baggage and provisions. My boots had not been off since the 13th, and I found it necessary to cut them to pieces, to get my swollen feet out of them.

This retreat terminated the campaign of 1812. After a few days' delay, and some requisite changes about the neighbourhood, while all the world were getting shook into their places, our battalion finally took possession of the village of Alameida for the winter, where, after forming a regimental mess, we detached an officer to Lamego, and secured to ourselves a bountiful supply of the best juice of the grape which the neighbouring banks of the Douro afforded. The quarter we now occupied was naturally pretty much upon a par with those of the last two winters, but it had the usual advantages attending the march of intellect. The officers of the division united in fitting up an empty chapel, in the village of Galegos, as an amateur theatre, for which, by the by, we were all regularly cursed, from the altar, by the bishop of Rodrigo. Lord Wellington kept a pack of foxhounds, and the Hon. Captain Stewart, of ours, a pack of harriers, so that these, in addition to our old *Bolero* meetings, enabled us to pass a very tolerable winter.

The neighbouring plains abounded with hares; it was one of the most beautiful coursing countries, perhaps, in the world; and there was, also, some shooting to be had at the numerous vultures preying on the dead carcasses which strewed the road-side on the line of our last retreat.

Up to this period Lord Wellington had been adored by the army, in consideration of his

K

brilliant achievements, and for his noble and
manly bearing in all things; but, in consequence
of some disgraceful irregularities which took
place during the retreat, he immediately after
issued an order, conveying a sweeping censure
on the whole army. His general conduct was
too upright for even the finger of malice itself
to point at; but as his censure, on this occasion,
was not strictly confined to the guilty, it afforded
a handle to disappointed persons, and excited a
feeling against him, on the part of individuals,
which has probably never since been obliterated.

It began by telling us that we had suffered
no privations; and, though this was hard to be
digested on an empty stomach, yet, taking it in
its more liberal meaning, that our privations
were not of an extent to justify any irregularities, which I readily admit; still, as many regiments were not guilty of any irregularities, it
is not to be wondered if such should have
felt, at first, a little sulky to find, in the general reproof, that no loop-hole whatever had
been left for them to creep through; for, I

believe I am justified in saying that neither our own, nor the two gallant corps associated with us, had a single man absent that we could not satisfactorily account for. But it touched us still more tenderly in not excepting us from his general charge of inexpertness in camp arrangements; for, it was *our belief*, and in which we were in some measure borne out by circumstances, that, had he placed us, at the same moment, in the same field, with an equal number of the best troops in France, that he would not only have seen our fires as quickly lit, but every Frenchman roasting on them to the bargain, if they waited long enough to be *dressed;* for there, perhaps, never was, nor ever again will be, such a war-brigade as that which was composed of the forty-third, fifty-second, and the rifles.

That not only censure, but condign punishment was merited, in many instances, is certain; and, had his lordship dismissed some officers from the service, and caused some of the disorderly soldiers to be shot, it would not only have been an act of justice, but, probably, a necessary

example.   Had he hanged every commissary,
too, who failed to issue the regular rations to the
troops dependent on him, unless they proved
that they were starved themselves, it would only
have been a just sacrifice to the offended sto-
machs of many thousands of gallant fellows.

In our brigade, I can safely say, that the order
in question excited " more of sorrow than of an
ger;" we thought that, had it been *particular*, it
would have been just; but, as it was *general*,
that it was inconsiderate; and we, therefore,
regretted that he who had been, and still was,
the god of our idolatry, should thereby have
laid himself open to the attacks of the ill-natured.

Alameida is a Spanish village, situated within
a stone's throw of the boundary-line of the
sister-kingdom; and, as the head-quarters of
the army, as well as the nearest towns, from
whence we drew our supplies, lay in Portugal,
our connexions, while we remained there, were
chiefly with the latter kingdom; and, having
passed the three last winters on their frontier,
we, in the month of May, 1813, prepared to

bid it a final adieu, with very little regret. The people were kind and hospitable, and not destitute of intelligence; but, somehow, they appeared to be the creatures of a former age, and showed an indolence and want of enterprise which marked them born for slaves; and, although the two cacadore regiments attached to our division were, at all times, in the highest order, and conducted themselves gallantly in the field, yet, I am of opinion that, as a nation, they owe their character for bravery almost entirely to the activity and gallantry of the British officers who organized and led them. The veriest cowards in existence must have shown the same front under such discipline. I did not see enough of their gentry to enable me to form an opinion about them; but the middling and lower orders are extremely filthy both in their persons and in their houses, and they have all an intolerable itch for gambling. The soldiers, though fainting with fatigue on the line of march, invariably group themselves in card-parties whenever they are allowed a few minutes'

halt ; and a non-commissioned officer, with half-
a-dozen men on any duty of fatigue, are very
generally to be seen as follows, viz. one man as
a sentry, to watch the approach of the superin-
tending officer, one man at work, and the non-
commissioned officer, with the other four, at
cards.

The cottages in Alameida, and, indeed, in all
the Spanish villages, generally contain two mud-
floored apartments : the outer one, though more
cleanly than the Irish, is, nevertheless, fashioned
after the same manner, and is common alike to
the pigs and the people ; while the inner looks
more like the gun-room of a ship-of-war, having
a sitting-apartment in the centre, with small
sleeping-cabins branching from it, each illuminated by a port-hole, about a foot square.
We did not see daylight "through a glass darkly,"
as on London's Ludgate-hill, for there the air
circulated freely, and mild it came, and pure,
and fragrant, as if it had just stolen over a bed
of roses. If a man did not like *that*, he had
only to shut his port, and remain in darkness,

inhaling his own preferred sweetness! The outside of my sleeping-cabin was interwoven with ivy and honeysuckle, and, among the branches, a nightingale had established itself, and sung sweetly, night after night, during the whole of the winter. I could not part from such a pleasing companion, and from a bed in which I had enjoyed so many tranquil slumbers, without a sigh, though I was ungrateful enough to accompany it with a fervent wish that I might never see them again; for I looked upon the period that I had spent there as so much time lost.

CHAP. XIII.

A Review. Assembly of the Army. March to Salamanca.
To Aldea Nueva. To Toro. An Affair of the Hussar Bri-
gade. To Palencia. To the Neighbourhood of Burgos.
To the Banks of the Ebro. Fruitful sleeping place. To
Medina. A Dance before it was due. Smell the Foe.
Affair at St. Milan. A Physical River.

May, 1813.—In the early part of this month
our division was reviewed by Lord Wellington,
preparatory to the commencement of another
campaign ; and I certainly never saw a body of
troops in a more highly-efficient state.   It did
one's very heart good to look at our battalion
that day, seeing each company standing a hundred strong, and the intelligence of several
campaigns stamped on each daring, bronzed
countenance, which looked you boldly in the

face, in the fullness of vigour and confidence, as if it cared neither for man nor devil.

On the 21st of May, our division broke up from winter-quarters, and assembled in front of Ciudad Rodrigo, with all excepting the left wing of the army, which, under Sir Thomas Graham, had already passed the Douro, and was ascending its right bank.

An army which has seen some campaigns in the field, affords a great deal of amusement in its assembling after winter-quarters. There is not only the greeting of long-parted friends and acquaintances in the same walks of life, but, among the different divisions which the nature of the service generally threw a good deal together, there was not so much as a mule or a donkey that was not known to each individual, and its absence noticed; nor a scamp of a boy, or a common Portuguese trull, who was not as particularly inquired after, as if the fate of the campaign depended on their presence.

On the 22d, we advanced towards Salamanca, and, the next day, halted at Samunoz, on our late field of action. With what different feelings did we now view the same spot! In our last visit, winter was on the face of the land, as well as on our minds; we were worn out with fatigue, mortification, and starvation; now, all was summer and sunshine. The dismal swamps had now become verdant meadows; we had plenty in the camp, vigour in our limbs, and hope in our bosoms.

We were, this day, joined by the household brigade of cavalry from England; and, as there was a report in the morning that the enemy were in the neighbourhood, some of the life-guards concluded that every thing in front of their camp must be a part of them, and they, accordingly, apprehended some of the light dragoon horses, which happened to be grazing near. One of their officers came to dine with me that day, and he was in the act of reporting their capture, when my orderly-book was brought at the moment, containing an offer of reward for the detection of the thieves!

On the 27th, we encamped on the banks of

the Tormes, at a ford, about a league below Salamanca. A body of the enemy, who had occupied the city, suffered severely before they got away, in a brush with some part of Sir Rowland Hill's corps; chiefly, I believe, from some of his artillery.

On the 28th, we crossed the river, and marched near to Aldea Nueva, where we remained stationary for some days, under Sir Rowland Hill; Lord Wellington having proceeded from Salamanca to join the left wing of the army, beyond the Douro.

On the 2d of June, we were again put in motion; and, after a very long march, encamped near the Douro, opposite the town of Toro.

Lord Wellington had arrived there the day before, without being opposed by the enemy; but there had been an affair of cavalry, a short distance beyond the town, in which the hussar brigade particularly distinguished themselves, and took about three hundred prisoners.

On the morning of the 3d, we crossed the river; and, marching through the town of

Toro, encamped about half a league beyond it.
The enemy had put the castle in a state of
repair, and constructed a number of other works
to defend the passage of the river ; but the mas-
terly eye of our chief, having seen his way round
the town, spared them the trouble of occupying
the works; yet, loth to think that so much labour should be altogether lost, he garrisoned
their castle with the three hundred taken by the
hussar brigade, for which it made a very good
jail.

On the 4th, we were again in motion, and had
a long, warm, fatiguing march ; as, also, on the
5th and 6th.   On the 7th, we encamped outside
of Palencia, a large rickety looking old town ;
with the front of every house supported by
pillars, like so many worn out old bachelors on
crutches.

The French did not interfere with our ac-
commodation in the slightest, but made it
a point to leave every place an hour or
two before we came to it; so that we quietly
continued our daily course, following nearly the

line of the Canal de Castile, through a country luxuriant in corn-fields and vineyards, until the 12th, when we arrived within two or three leagues of Burgos, (on its left,) and where we found a body of the enemy in position, whom we immediately proceeded to attack ; but they evaporated on our approach, and fell back upon Burgos. We encamped for the night on the banks of a river, a short distance to the rear. Next morning, at daylight, an explosion shook the ground like an earthquake, and made every man jump upon his legs ; and it was not until some hours after, when Lord Wellington returned from reconnoitring, that we learnt that the castle of Burgos had been just blown up, and the town evacuated by the enemy.

We continued our march on the 13th, through a very rich country.

On the 14th, we had a long harassing day's march, through a rugged mountainous country, which afforded only an occasional glimpse of fertility, in some pretty little valleys with which it was intersected.

We started at daylight on the 15th, through a dreary region of solid rock, bearing an abundant crop of loose stones, without a particle of soil or vegetation visible to the naked eye in any direction. After leaving nearly twenty miles of this horrible wilderness behind us, our weary minds clogged with an imaginary view of nearly as much more of it in our front, we found ourselves, all at once, looking down upon the valley of the Ebro, near the village of Arenas, one of the richest, loveliest, and most romantic spots that I ever beheld. The influence of such a scene on the mind can scarcely be believed. Five minutes before we were all as *lively* as stones. In a moment we were all fruits and flowers; and many a pair of legs, that one would have thought had not a kick left in them, were, in five minutes after, seen dancing across the bridge, to the tune of " the downfal of Paris," which struck up from the bands of the different regiments.

I lay down that night in a cottage garden, with my head on a melon, and my eye on a cherry-tree, and resigned myself to a repose which did not require a long courtship.

We resumed our march at daybreak on the 16th. The road, in the first instance, wound through orchards and luxurious gardens, and then closed in to the edge of the river, through a difficult and formidable pass, where the rocks on each side, arising to a prodigious height, hung over each other in fearful grandeur, and in many places nearly met together over our heads.

After following the course of the river for nearly two miles, the rocks on each side gradually expanded into another valley, lovely as the one we had left, and where we found the fifth division of our army lying encamped. They were still asleep; and the rising sun, and a beautiful morning, gave additional sublimity to the scene; for there was nothing but the tops of the white tents peeping above the fruit trees; and an occasional sentinel pacing his post, that gave any indication of what a nest of hornets the blast of a bugle could bring out of that apparently peaceful solitude.

Our road now wound up the mountain to our right; and, almost satiated with the continued grandeur around us, we arrived, in the afternoon, at the town of Medina, and encamped a short distance beyond it.

We were welcomed into every town or village through which we passed, by the peasant girls, who were in the habit of meeting us with garlands of flowers, and dancing before us in a peculiar style of their own; and it not unfrequently happened, that while they were so employed with one regiment, the preceding one was diligently engaged in pulling down some of their houses for firewood—a measure which we were sometimes obliged to have recourse to, where no other fuel could be had, and for which they were, ultimately, paid by the British Government; but it was a measure that was more likely to have set the poor souls dancing mad than for joy, had they foreseen the consequences of our visit.

June 17th.—We had not seen any thing of the enemy since we left the neighbourhood of

Burgos; but, after reaching our ground this evening, we were aware that some of their videttes were feeling for us.

On the morning of the 18th, we were ordered to march to San Milan, a small town, about two leagues off; and where, on our arrival on the hill above it, we found a division of French infantry, as strong as ourselves, in the act of crossing our path. The surprise, I believe, was mutual, though I doubt whether the pleasure was equally so; for we were red hot for an opportunity of retaliating for the Salamanca retreat; and, as the old saying goes, " there is no opportunity like the present." Their leading brigade had nearly passed before we came up, but not a moment was lost after we did. Our battalion dispersing among the brushwood, went down the hill upon them; and, with a destructive fire, broke through their line of march, supported by the rest of the brigade. Those that had passed made no attempt at a stand, but continued their flight, keeping up as good a fire as their circumstances would permit; while we kept hanging on their flank and rear, through a good rifle country, which enabled us to make considerable havoc among them. Their general's aide-de-camp, amongst others, was mortally wounded; and a lady, on a white horse, who probably was his wife, remained beside him, until we came very near. She appeared to be in great distress; but, though we called to her to remain, and not to be alarmed, yet she galloped off as soon as a decided step became necessary. The object of her solicitude did not survive many minutes after we reached him. We followed the retreating foe until late in the afternoon. On this occasion, our brigade came in for all the blows, and the other for all the baggage, which was marching between the two French brigades; the latter of which, seeing the scrape into which the first had fallen, very prudently left it to its fate, and dispersed on the opposite mountains, where some of them fell into the hands of a Spanish force that was detached in pursuit; but, I believe, the greater part succeeded in joining their army the day after the battle of Vittoria.

We heard a heavy cannonade all day to our left, occasioned, as we understood, by the fifth division falling in with another detachment of the enemy, which the unexpected and rapid movements of Lord Wellington was hastening to their general point of assembly.

On the early part of the 19th, we were fagging up the face of a mountain, under a sultry hot sun, until we came to a place where a beautiful clear stream was dashing down the face of it; when the division was halted, to enable the men to refresh themselves. Every man carries a cup, and every man ran and swallowed a cup full of it—it was salt water from the springs of Salinas; and it was truly ludicrous to see their faces after taking such a voluntary dose. I observed an Irishman, who, not satisfied with the first trial, and believing that his cup had been infected by some salt breaking loose in his haversack, he washed it carefully and then drank a second

one, when, finding no change, he exclaimed,—
" by J—-s, boys, we must be near the sea, for
the water's getting salt !" We, soon after,
passed through the village of Salinas, situated at
the source of the stream, where there is a considerable salt manufactory. The inhabitants were
so delighted to see us, that they placed buckets
full of it at the doors of the different houses, and
entreated our men to help themselves as they
passed along. It rained hard in the afternoon,
and it was late before we got to our ground.
We heard a good deal of firing in the neighbourhood in the course of the day, but our division
was not engaged.

We retained the same bivouac all day on the
20th ; it was behind a range of mountains within
a short distance of the left of the enemy's position, as we afterwards discovered ; and though
we heard an occasional gun, from the other side
of the mountain in the course of the day, fired
at Lord Wellington's reconnoitring party, the
peace of our valley remained undisturbed.

CHAP. XIV.

Battle of Vittoria. Defeat of the Enemy. Confusion among their Followers. Plunder. Colonel Cameron. Pursuit, and the Capture of their Last Gun. Arrive near Pampeluna. At Villalba. An Irish method of making a useless Bed useful.

BATTLE OF VITTORIA.

June 21st, 1813.

Our division got under arms this morning before daylight, passed the base of the mountain by its left, through the camp of the fourth division, who were still asleep in their tents, to the banks of the river Zadora, at the village of Tres Puentes. The opposite side of the river was occupied by the enemy's advanced posts, and we saw their army on the hills beyond, while the spires of Vittoria were visible in the distance. We felt as if there was likely to be a battle; but as that was an event we were never sure of, until we found ourselves actually in it, we lay for some time just out of musket shot, uncertain what was likely to turn up, and waiting for orders. At length a sharp fire of musketry was heard to our right; and, on looking in that direction, we saw the head of Sir Rowland Hill's corps, together with some Spanish troops, attempting to force the mountain which marked the enemy's left. The three battalions of our regiment were, at the same moment, ordered forward to feel the enemy, who lined the opposite banks of the river, with whom we were quickly engaged in a warm skirmish. The affair with Sir Rowland Hill became gradually warmer, but ours had apparently no other object than to amuse those who were opposite to us, for the moment; so that, for about two hours longer, it seemed as if there would be nothing but an affair of outposts. About twelve o'clock, however, we were moved rapidly to our

left, followed by the rest of the division, till
we came to an abrupt turn of the river, where we
found a bridge, unoccupied by the enemy, which
we immediately crossed, and took possession of,
what appeared to me to be, an old field-work,
on the other side. We had not been many
seconds there before we observed the bayonets
of the third and seventh divisions glittering
above the standing corn, and advancing upon
another bridge, which stood about a quarter of a
mile further to our left, and where, on their
arrival, they were warmly opposed by the
enemy's light troops, who lined the bank of the
river, (which we ourselves were now on,) in
great force, for the defence of the bridge. As
soon as this was observed by our division,
Colonel Barnard advanced with our battalion,
and took them in flank with such a furious fire
as quickly dislodged them, and thereby opened
a passage for these two divisions free of expense,
which must otherwise have cost them dearly.
What with the rapidity of our movement, the
colour of our dress, and our close contact with

the enemy, before they would abandon their post, we had the misfortune to be identified with them for some time, by a battery of our own guns, who, not observing the movement, continued to serve it out indiscriminately, and all the while admiring their practice upon us; nor was it until the red coats of the third division joined us, that they discovered their mistake.

The battle now commenced in earnest; and this was perhaps the most interesting moment of the whole day. Sir Thomas Graham's artillery, with the first and fifth divisions, began to be heard far to our left, beyond Vittoria. The bridge, which we had just cleared, stood so near to a part of the enemy's position, that the seventh division was instantly engaged in close action with them at that point.

On the mountain to our extreme right the action continued to be general and obstinate, though we observed that the enemy were giving ground slowly to Sir Rowland Hill. The passage of the river by our division had turned the enemy's outpost, at the bridge, on our right,

where we had been engaged in the morning, and
they were now retreating, followed by the fourth
division. The plain between them and Sir
Rowland Hill was occupied by the British cavalry,
who were now seen filing out of a wood, squadron
after squadron, galloping into form as they gradually cleared it. The hills behind were covered
with spectators, and the third and the light
divisions, covered by our battalion, advanced
rapidly, upon a formidable hill, in front of the
enemy's centre, which they had neglected to
occupy in sufficient force.

In the course of our progress, our men kept
picking off the French videttes, who were
imprudent enough to hover too near us; and
many a horse, bounding along the plain, drag-
ging his late rider by the stirrup-irons, contributed in making it a scene of extraordinary and
exhilarating interest.

Old Picton rode at the head of the third
division, dressed in a blue coat and a round hat,
and swore as roundly all the way as if he had
been wearing two cocked ones. Our battalion

L

soon cleared the hill in question of the enemy's
light troops; but we were pulled up on the
opposite side of it by one of their lines, which
occupied a wall at the entrance of a village
immediately under us.   During the few minutes
that we stopped there, while a brigade of the
third division was deploying into line, two of
our companies lost two officers and thirty men,
chiefly from the fire of artillery bearing on
the spot from the French position.   One of
their shells burst immediately under my nose,
part of it struck my boot and stirrup-iron, and
the rest of it kicked up such a dust about me
that my charger refused to obey orders; and,
while I was spurring and he capering, I heard a
voice behind me, which I knew to be Lord Wellington's, calling out, in a tone of reproof, " look
to keeping your men together, sir;" and though,
God knows, I had not the remotest idea that he
was within a mile of me at the time, yet, so
sensible was I that circumstances warranted his
supposing that I was a young officer, cutting a
caper, by way of bravado, before him, that

worlds would not have tempted me to look round at the moment. The French fled from the wall as soon as they received a volley from a part of the third division, and we instantly dashed down the hill, and charged them through the village, capturing three of their guns; the first, I believe, that were taken that day. They received a reinforcement, and drove us back before our supports could come to our assistance; but, in the scramble of the moment, our men were knowing enough to cut the traces, and carry off the horses, so that, when we retook the village, immediately after, the guns still remained in our possession. The battle now became general along the whole line, and the cannonade was tremendous. At one period, we held on one side of a wall, near the village, while the French were on the other, so that any person who chose to put his head over from either side was sure of getting a sword or a bayonet up his nostrils. This situation was, of course, too good to be of long endurance. The victory, I believe, was never for a moment doubtful. The enemy were so completely out-generalled, and the superiority of our troops was such, that to carry their positions required little more than the time necessary to march to them. After forcing their centre, the fourth division and our own got on the flank and rather in rear of the enemy's left wing, who were retreating before Sir Rowland Hill, and who, to effect their escape, were now obliged to fly in one confused mass. Had a single regiment of our dragoons been at hand, or even a squadron, to have forced them into shape for a few minutes, we must have taken from ten to twenty thousand prisoners. After marching along side of them for nearly two miles, and as a disorderly body will always move faster than an orderly one, we had the mortification to see them gradually heading us, until they finally made their escape. I have no doubt but that our mounted gentlemen were doing their duty as they ought in another part of the field; yet, it was impossible to deny ourselves the satisfaction of cursing them all, because a portion had not been there at such a critical moment. Our elevated situation, at this time, afforded a good view of the field of battle to our left, and I could not help being struck with an unusual appearance of unsteadiness and want of confidence among the French troops. I saw a dense mass of many thousands occupying a good defensible post, who gave way in the greatest confusion, before a single line of the third division, almost without feeling them. If there was nothing in any other part of the position to justify the movement, and I do not think there was, they ought to have been flogged, every man, from the general downwards.

The ground was particularly favourable to the retreating foe, as every half-mile afforded a fresh and formidable position, so that, from the commencement of the action to the city of Vittoria, a distance of six or eight miles, we were involved in one continued hard skirmish. On passing Vittoria, however, the scene became quite new and infinitely more amusing, as the French had made no provision for a retreat; and, Sir Thomas Graham having seized upon the great road to France, the only one left open was that leading by Pampeluna; and it was not open long, for their fugitive army, and their myriads of followers, with baggage, guns, carriages, &c. being all precipitated upon it at the same moment, it got choked up about a mile beyond the town, in the most glorious state of confusion; and the drivers, finding that one pair of legs was worth two pair of wheels, abandoned it all to the victors.

Many of their followers who had light carriages, endeavoured to make their escape through the fields; but it only served to prolong their misery.

I shall never forget the first that we overtook: it was in the midst of a stubble-field, for some time between us and the French skirmishers, the driver doing all he could to urge the horses along; but our balls began to whistle so plentifully about his ears, that he at last dismounted in despair, and, getting on his knees, under the carriage, began praying. His place on the box was quickly occupied by as many of our fellows

as could stick on it, while others were scrambling
in at the doors on each side, and not a few
on the roof, handling the baskets there so
roughly, as to occasion loud complaints from the
fowls within. I rode up to the carriage, to see
that the people inside were not improperly
treated ; but the only one there was an old gouty
gentleman, who, from the nature of his cargo,
must either have robbed his own house, or that
of a very good fellow, for the carriage was literally laden with wines and provisions. Never
did victors make a more legal or useful capture ;
for it was now six in the evening, and it had
evidently been the old gentleman's fault if he
had not already dined, whereas it was our misfortune, rather than our fault, that we had not
tasted anything since three o'clock in the morning,
so that when one of our men knocked the neck
off a bottle, and handed it to me, to take a drink,
I nodded to the old fellow's health, and drank it
off without the smallest scruple of conscience.
It was excellent claret, and if he still lives to
tell the story, I fear he will not give us the

credit of having belonged to such a *civil* depart-
ment as his appeared.

We did not cease the pursuit until dark, and
then halted in a field of wheat, about two miles
beyond Vittoria. The victory was complete.
They carried off only one howitzer out of their
numerous artillery, which, with baggage, stores,
provisions, money, and every thing that con-
stitutes the *matériel* of an army, fell into our
hands.

It is much to be lamented, on those occasions,
that the people who contribute most to the victory should profit the least by it; not that I am
an advocate for plunder—on the contrary, I
would much rather that all our fighting was for
pure *love;* but, as every thing of value falls into
the hands of the followers, and scoundrels who
skulk from the ranks for the double purpose of
plundering and saving their dastardly carcasses,
what I regret is, that the man who deserts his
post should thereby have an opportunity of en-
riching himself with impunity, while the true
man gets nothing; but the evil I believe is irre-

mediable. Sir James Kempt, who commanded our brigade, in passing one of the captured waggons in the evening, saw a soldier loading himself with money, and was about to have him conveyed to the camp as a prisoner, when the fellow begged hard to be released, and to be allowed to retain what he had got, telling the general that all the boxes in the waggon were filled with gold. Sir James, with his usual liberality, immediately adopted the idea of securing it, as a reward to his brigade, for their gallantry; and, getting a fatigue party, he caused the boxes to be removed to his tent, and ordered an officer and some men from each regiment to parade there next morning, to receive their proportions of it; but, when they opened the boxes, they found them filled with *hammers, nails, and horse-shoes!*

Among the evil chances of that glorious day, I had to regret the temporary loss of Colonel Cameron,—a bad wound in the thigh having obliged him to go to England. Of him I can truly say, that, as a *friend*, his heart was in the right place, and, as a *soldier*, his right place was at the head of a regiment in the face of an enemy. I never saw an officer feel more at home in such a situation, nor do I know any one who could fill it better.

A singular accident threw me in the way of a dying French officer, who gave me a group of family portraits to transmit to his friends; but, as it was not until the following year that I had an opportunity of making the necessary inquiries after them, they had then left their residence, and were nowhere to be heard of.

As not only the body, but the mind, had been in constant occupation since three o'clock in the morning, circumstances no sooner permitted (about ten at night) than I threw myself on the ground, and fell into a profound sleep, from which I did not awake until broad daylight, when I found a French soldier squatted near me, intensely watching for the opening of my *shutters*. He had contrived to conceal himself there during the night; and, when he saw that I was awake, he immediately jumped

on his legs, and very obsequiously presented me
with a map of France, telling me that as there
was now a probability of our visiting his native
country, he could make himself very useful,
and would be glad if I would accept of his
services. I thought it unfair, however, to de-
prive him of the present opportunity of seeing a
little more of the world himself, and, therefore,
sent him to join the rest of the prisoners, which
would insure him a trip to England, free of
expense.

About midday, on the 22d, our three battalions, with some cavalry and artillery, were
ordered in pursuit of the enemy.

I do not know how it is, but I have always
had a mortal objection to be killed the day after
a victory. In the actions preceding a battle, or
in the battle itself, it never gave me much uneasiness, as being all in the way of business; but,
after surviving the great day, I always felt as if
I had a right to live to tell the story; and I,
therefore, did not find the ensuing three days'

fighting half so pleasant as they otherwise would have been.

Darkness overtook us this night without our overtaking the enemy; and we halted in a grove of pines, exposed to a very heavy rain. In imprudently shifting my things from one tree to another, after dark, some rascal contrived to steal the velisse containing my dressing things, than which I do not know a greater loss, when there is no possibility of replacing any part of them.

We overtook their rear-guard early on the following day, and, hanging on their line of march until dark, we did them all the mischief that we could. They burnt every village through which they passed, under the pretence of impeding our movements; but, as it did not make the slightest difference in that respect, we could only view it as a wanton piece of cruelty.

On the 24th, we were again engaged in pressing their rear the greater part of the day; and, ultimately, in giving them the last kick, under the walls of Pampeluna, where we had the glory of capturing their last gun, which literally sent them into France without a single piece of ordnance.

Our battalion occupied, that night, a large, well-furnished, but uninhabited chateau, a short distance from Pampeluna.

We got under arms early on the morning of the 25th; and, passing by a mountain-path, to the left of Pampeluna, within range of the guns, though they did not fire at us, circled the town, until we reached the village of Villalba, where we halted for the night. Since I joined that army, I had never, up to that period, been master of any thing in the shape of a bed; and, though I did not despise a bundle of straw, when it could conveniently be had, yet my boat-cloak and blanket were more generally to be seen, spread out for my reception on the bare earth. But, in proceeding to turn into them, as usual, this evening, I was not a little astonished to find, in their stead, a comfortable mattress, with a suitable supply of linen, blankets, and pillows; in short, the very identical bedding on

which I had slept, the night before, in the chateau, three leagues off, and which my rascal of
an Irishman had bundled altogether on the back
of my mule, without giving me the slightest hint
of his intentions. On my taking him to task
about it, and telling him that he would certainly
be hanged, all that he said in reply was, " by
J—s, they had more than a hundred beds in
that house, and not a single soul to sleep in them."
I was very much annoyed, at the time, that there
was no possibility of returning them to their
rightful owner, as, independent of its being
nothing short of a regular robbery, I really
looked upon them as a very unnecessary encum-
brance; but being forced, in some measure, to
indulge in their comforts, I was not long in
changing my mind; and was, ultimately, not
very sorry that the possibility of restoration never
did occur.

CHAP. XV.

March to intercept Clausel. Tafalla. Olite. The dark End
of a Night March to Casada. Clausel's Escape. Sanguessa. My Tent struck. Return to Villalba. Weighty
Considerations on Females. St. Esteban. A Severe
Dance. Position at Bera. Soult's Advance, and Battle
of the Pyrenees. His Defeat and subsequent Actions.
A Morning's Ride.

June 26th, 1813.—OUR division fell in this
morning, at daylight, and, marching out of
Villalba, circled round the southern side of
Pampeluna, until we reached the great road leading to Tafalla, where we found ourselves united
with the third and fourth divisions, and a large
body of cavalry; the whole under the immediate command of Lord Wellington, proceeded
southward, with a view to intercept General

Clausel, who, with a strong division of the French army, had been at Logrona, on the day of the battle of Vittoria, and was now endeavouring to pass into the Pyrenees by our right. We marched until sun set, and halted for the night in a wood.

On the morning of the 27th we were again in motion, and passing through a country abounding in fruits, and all manner of delightful prospects ; and through the handsome town of Tafalla, where we were enthusiastically cheered by the beauteous occupants of the numerous balconies overhanging the streets. We halted, for the night, in an olive-grove, a short distance from Olite.

At daylight next morning we passed through the town of Olite, and continued our route until we began to enter among the mountains, about mid-day, when we halted two hours, to enable the men to cook, and again resumed our march. Darkness overtook us, while struggling through a narrow rugged road, which wound its way along the bank of the Arragon ; and we did not reach our destination, at Casada, until near midnight, where, amid torrents of rain, and in the darkness of the night, we could find nothing but ploughed fields on which to repose our weary limbs, nor could we find a particle of fuel to illuminate the cheerless scene.

> Breathed there a man of soul so dead,
> Who would not to himself have said,
> This is——a confounded comfortless dwelling.

Dear Sir Walter,—pray excuse the *Casadians*, from your curse entailed on home haters, for if any one of them ever succeeds in getting beyond the mountain, by the road which I traversed, he ought to be anathematized if ever he seek his home again.

We passed the whole of the next day in the same place. It was discovered that Clausel had been walking blindly into the *lion's den*, when the *alcaldé* of a neighbouring village had warned him of his danger, and he was thereby enabled to avoid us, by turning off towards Zaragossa. We heard that Lord Wellington had caused the informer to be hanged. I hope he did, but I don't believe it.

On the 30th we began to retrace our steps to Pampeluna, in the course of which we halted two nights at Sanguessa, a populous mountain town, full of old rattle-trap houses, a good many of which we pulled down for firewood, by way of making room for improvements.

I was taking advantage of this extra day's halt to communicate to my friends the important events of the past fortnight, when I found myself all at once wrapped into a bundle, with my tent-pole, and sent rolling upon the earth, mixed up with my portable table and writing utensils, while the devil himself seemed to be dancing a hornpipe over my body! Although this is a sort of thing that one will sometimes submit to, when it comes by way of illusion, at its proper time and place, such as a midnight visit from a night-mare; yet, as I seemed now to be visited by a horse as well as a mare, and that, too, in the middle of the day, and in the midst of a crowded camp, it was rather too much of a joke, and I therefore sung out most lustily. I was not long in getting extricated, and found that the whole scene had been arranged by two rascally donkies, who, in a frolicsome humour, had been chasing each other about the neighbourhood, until they finally tumbled into my tent, with a force which drew every peg, and rolled the whole of it over on the top of me! It might have been good sport to them, but it was none to me!

On the 3d of July, we resumed our quarters in Villalba, where we halted during the whole of the next day; and were well supplied with fish, fresh-butter, and eggs, brought by the peasantry of Biscay, who are the most *manly* set of *women* that I ever saw. They are very square across the shoulders; and, what between the quantity of fish, and the quantity of yellow petticoats, they carry a load which an ordinary mule might boast of.

A division of Spaniards having relieved us in

the blockade of Pampeluna, our division, on the 5th of July, advanced into the Pyrenees.

On the 7th, we took up our quarters in the little town of St. Esteban, situated in a lovely valley, watered by the Bidassoa. The different valleys in the Pyrenees are very rich and fertile. The towns are clean and regular, and the natives very handsome. They are particularly smart about the limbs, and in no other part of the world have I seen any thing, natural or artificial, to rival the complexions of the ladies, *i. e.* to the admirers of pure red and white.

We were allowed to remain several days in this enchanting spot, and enjoyed ourselves exceedingly. They had an extraordinary style of dancing, peculiar to themselves. At a particular part of the tune, they all began thumping the floor with their feet, as hard and as fast as they were able, not in the shape of a figure or flourish of any kind, but even down pounding. I could not, myself, see any thing either graceful or difficult in the operation; but they seemed to think that there was only one lady amongst them who

could do it in perfection; she was the wife of a
French Colonel, and had been left in the care of
her friends, (and his enemies): she certainly
could pound the ground both harder and faster
than any one there, eliciting the greatest ap-
plause after every performance; and yet I do not
think that she could have caught a *French*
husband by her superiority in that particular
step.

After our few days halt, we advanced along
the banks of the Bidassoa, through a succession of beautiful little fertile valleys, thickly
studded with clean respectable looking farm-
houses and little villages, and bounded by stupendous, picturesque, and well wooded mountains, until we came to the hill next to the
village of Bera, which we found occupied by a
small force of the enemy, who, after receiving
a few shots from our people, retired through
the village into their position behind it. Our
line of demarcation was then clearly seen. The
mountain which the French army occupied was
the last ridge of the Pyrenees; and their sentries

stood on the face of it, within pistol shot of the village of Bera, which now became the advanced post of our division. The Bidassoa takes a sudden turn to the left at Bera, and formed a natural boundary between the two armies from thence to the sea; but all to our right was open, and merely marked a continuation of the valley of Bera, which was a sort of neutral ground, in which the French foragers and our own frequently met and helped themselves, in the greatest good humour, while any forage remained, without exchanging either words or blows. The left wing of the army, under Sir Thomas Graham, now commenced the siege of St. Sebastian; and as Lord Wellington had, at the same time, to cover both that and the blockade of Pampeluna, our army occupied an extended position of many miles.

Marshal Soult having succeeded to the command of the French army, and finding, towards the end of July, that St. Sebastian was about to be stormed, and that the garrison of Pampeluna were beginning to get on short allowance, he determined on making a bold push for the relief of both places; and, assembling the whole of his army, he forced the pass of Maya, and advanced rapidly upon Pampeluna. Lord Wellington was never to be caught napping. His army occupied too extended a position to offer effectual resistance at any of their advanced posts; but, by the time that Marshal Soult had worked his way up to the last ridge of the Pyrenees, and within sight of " the haven of " his wishes," he found his lordship waiting for him, with four divisions of the army, who treated him to one of the most signal and sanguinary defeats that he ever experienced.

Our division, during the important movements on our right, was employed in keeping up the communication between the troops under the immediate command of Lord Wellington and those under Sir Thomas Graham, at St. Sebastian. We retired, the first day, to the mountains behind Le Secca; and, just as we were about to lie down for the night, we were again ordered under arms, and continued our retreat in utter darkness, through a mountain path, where, in many places, a false step might have rolled a fellow as far as the other world. The consequence was, that, although we were kept on our legs during the whole of the night, we found, when daylight broke, that the tail of the column had not got a quarter of a mile from their starting-post.

On a good broad road it is all very well; but, on a narrow bad road, a night march is like a night-mare, harassing a man to no purpose.

On the 26th, we occupied a ridge of mountain near enough to hear the battle, though not in a situation to see it; and remained the whole of the day in the greatest torture, for want of news. About midnight we heard the joyful tidings of the enemy's defeat, with the loss of four thousand prisoners. Our division proceeded in pursuit, at daylight, on the following morning.

We moved rapidly by the same road on which we had retired; and, after a forced march, found ourselves; when near sun-set, on the flank of their retiring column, on the Bidassoa, near the bridge of Janca, and immediately proceeded to business.

The sight of a Frenchman always acted like a cordial on the spirits of a rifleman ; and the fatigues of the day were forgotten, as our three battalions extended among the brushwood, and went down to " knock the dust out of their " hairy knapsacks,"* as our men were in the habit of expressing themselves; but, in place of knocking the dust out of them, I believe that most of their knapsacks were knocked in the dust; for the greater part of those who were not *floored* along with their knapsacks, shook them off, by way of enabling the owner to make a smarter scramble across that portion of the road on which our leaden shower was pouring ; and, foes as they were, it was impossible not to feel a degree of pity for their situation: pressed by an enemy in the rear, an inaccessible moun-tain on their right, and a river on their left, lined by an invisible foe, from whom there was

---

* The French knapsack is made of unshorn goat-skin.

M

no escape, but the desperate one of running the
gauntlet.   However, " as every —— has his
" day," and this was ours, we must stand ex-
cused for making the most of it.   Each company, as they passed, gave us a volley ; but as
they had nothing to guide their aim, except the
smoke from our rifles, we had very few men hit.

Amongst other papers found on the road that
night, one of our officers discovered the letter-
book of the French military secretary, with his
correspondence included to the day before.   It
was immediately sent to Lord Wellington.

We advanced, next morning, and occupied our
former post, at Bera.   The enemy still continued
to hold the mountain of Echelar, which, as it rose
out of the right end of our ridge, was, properly
speaking, a part of our property ; and we concluded, that a sense of justice would have
induced them to leave it of their own accord in
the course of the day; but when, towards the
afternoon, they shewed no symptoms of quitting,
our division, leaving their kettles on the fire,
proceeded to eject them.   As we approached

the mountain, the peak of it caught a passing cloud, that gradually descended in a thick fog, and excluded them from our view. Our three battalions, however, having been let loose, under Colonel Barnard, we soon made ourselves " Children of the Mist;" and, guided to our opponents by the whistling of their balls, made them descend from their " high " estate;" and, handing them across the valley into their own position, we then retired to ours, where we found our tables ready spread, and a comfortable dinner waiting for us.

This was one of the most gentleman-like day's fighting that I ever experienced, although we had to lament the vacant seats of one or two of our messmates.

August 22d.—I narrowly escaped being taken prisoner this morning, very foolishly. A division of Spaniards occupied the ground to our left, beyond the Bidassoa; and, having mounted my horse to take a look at their post, I passed through a small village, and then got on a rugged path winding along the edge of the

river, where I expected to find their outposts.
The river, at that place, was not above knee-
deep, and about ten or twelve yards across; and
though I saw a number of soldiers gathering
chestnuts from a row of trees which lined the
opposite bank, I concluded that they were
Spaniards, and kept moving onwards; but, observing, at last, that I was an object of greater
curiosity than I ought to be, to people who had
been in the daily habit of seeing the uniform,
it induced me to take a more particular look at
my neighbours; when, to my consternation, I
saw the French eagle ornamenting the front of
every cap. I instantly wheeled my horse to the
right about; and seeing that I had a full quarter
of a mile to traverse at a walk, before I could
get clear of them, I began to whistle, with as
much unconcern as I could muster, while my
eye was searching, like lightning, for the means
of escape, in the event of their trying to cut me
off. I had soon the satisfaction of observing
that none of them had firelocks, which reduced
my capture to the chances of a race; for, though

the hill on my right was inaccessible to a horseman, it was not so to a dismounted Scotchman; and I, therefore, determined, in case of necessity, to abandon my horse, and shew them what I could do on my own bottom at a pinch. Fortunately, they did not attempt it; and I could scarcely credit my good luck, when I found myself once more in my own tent.

CHAP. XVI.

THE 25th of August, being our regimental
anniversary, was observed by the officers of our
three battalions with all due conviviality. Two
trenches, calculated to accommodate seventy
gentlemen's legs, were dug in the green sward;
the earth between them stood for a table, and
behind was our seat, and though the table

could not boast of *all* the delicacies of a civic entertainment, yet

" The worms they crept in, and the worms they crept out,"

As the earth almost quaked with the weight of the feast, and the enemy certainly did, from the noise of it. For so many fellows holding such precarious tenures of their lives could not meet together in commemoration of such an event, without indulging in an occasional cheer—not a whispering cheer, but one that echoed far and wide into the French lines, and as it was a sound that had often pierced them before, and never yet boded them any good, we heard afterwards that they were kept standing at their arms the greater part of the night in consequence.

At the time of Soult's last irruption into the Pyrenees, Sir Thomas Graham had made an unsuccessful attempt to carry St. Sebastian b storm, and having, ever since, been prosecuting the siege with unremitting vigour, the works were now reduced to such a state as to justify a second attempt, and our division sent forth their three hundred volunteers to join the storming party.* The morning on which we expected the assault to take place, we had turned out before day-light, as usual, and as a thick fog hung on the French position, which prevented our seeing them, we turned in again at the usual time, but had scarcely done so, when the mist rode off on a passing breeze, showing us the opposite hills bristling with their bayonets, and their columns descending rapidly towards us. The bugles instantly sounded to arms, and we formed on our alarm posts. We thought at first that the attack was intended for us, but they presently began to pass the river, a little below the village of Bera, and to advance against the Spaniards on our left. They were covered by some mountain guns, from which their first shell fell short, and made such

* Lieutenants Percival and Hamilton commanded those from our battalion, and were both desperately wounded.

a breach in their own leading column, that we could not resist giving three cheers to their marksman. Leaving a strong covering party to keep our division in check at the bridge of Bera, their main body followed the Spaniards, who, offering little opposition, continued retiring towards St. Sebastian.

We remained quiet the early part of the day, under a harmless fire from their mountain guns; but, towards the afternoon, our battalion, with part of the forty-third, and supported by a brigade of Spaniards, were ordered to pass by the bridge of Le Secca, and to move in a parallel direction with the French, along the same ridge of hills.

The different flanking-posts of the enemy permitted the forty-third and us to pass them quietly, thinking, I suppose, that it was their interest to keep the peace; but not so with the Spaniards, whom they kept in a regular fever, under a smart fire, the whole way. We took up a position at dark, on a pinnacle of the same mountain, within three or four hundred yards of them. There had been a heavy firing all day to our left, and we heard, in the course of the night, of the fall of St. Sebastian, as well as of the defeat of the force which we had seen following the Spaniards in that direction.

As we always took the liberty of abusing our friends, the commissaries, whether with or without reason, whenever we happened to be on short allowance, it is but fair to say that when our supporting Spanish brigadier came to compare notes with us here, we found that we had three days' rations in the haversack against his none. He very politely proposed to relieve us from half of ours, and to give a receipt for it, but we told him that the trouble in carrying it was a pleasure !

At day-light next morning we found that the enemy had altogether disappeared from our front. The heavy rains during the past night had rendered the Bidassoa no longer fordable, and the bridge of Bera being the only retreat left open, it was fortunate for them that they took advantage of it before we had time to occupy the post with a sufficient force to defend the passage, otherwise they would have been compelled, in all probability, to have laid down their arms.

As it was, they suffered very severely from two companies of our second battalion, who were on piquet there. The two captains commanding them were, however, killed in the affair.

We returned in the course of the day and resumed our post at Bera, the enemy continuing to hold theirs beyond it.

The ensuing month passed by, without producing the slightest novelty, and we began to get heartily tired of our situation. Our souls, in fact, were strung for war, and peace afforded no enjoyment, unless the place did, and there was none to be found in a valley of the Pyrenees, which the ravages of contending armies had reduced to a desert. The labours of the French on the opposite mountain had, in the first instance, been confined to fortification; but, as the season advanced, they seemed to think that the branch of a tree, or a sheet of

canvass, was too slender a barrier between them
and a frosty night, and their fortified camp was
gradually becoming a fortified town, of regular
brick and mortar. Though we were living under the influence of the same sky, we did not
think it necessary to give ourselves the same
trouble, but reasoned on their proceedings like
philosophers, and calculated, from the aspect of
the times, that there was a probability of a
speedy transfer of property, and that it might
still be reserved for us to give their town a
name; nor were we disappointed. Late on the
night of the 7th of October, Colonel Barnard
arrived from head-quarters, with the intelligence that the next was to be the day of trial.
Accordingly, on the morning of the 8th, the
fourth division came up to support us, and we
immediately marched down to the foot of the
enemy's position, shook off our knapsacks before their faces, and went at them.

The action commenced by five companies of
our third battalion advancing, under Colonel
Ross, to dislodge the enemy from a hill which

they occupied in front of their entrenchments; and there never was a movement more beautifully executed, for they walked quietly and steadily up, and swept them regularly off without firing a single shot until the enemy had turned their backs, when they then served them out with a most destructive discharge. The movement excited the admiration of all who witnessed it, and added another laurel to the already crowded wreath which adorned the name of that distinguished officer.

At the first look of the enemy's position, it appeared as if our brigade had got the most difficult task to perform ; but, as the capture of this hill showed us a way round the flank of their entrenchments, we carried one after the other, until we finally gained the summit, with very little loss. Our second brigade, however, were obliged to take " the bull by the horns," on their side, and suffered more severely ; but they rushed at every thing with a determination that defied resistance, carrying redoubt after redoubt at the point of the bayonet, until they finally joined us on the summit of the mountain, with three hundred prisoners in their possession.

We now found ourselves firmly established within the French territory, with a prospect before us that was truly refreshing, considering that we had not seen the sea for three years, and that our views, for months, had been confined to fogs and the peaks of mountains. On our left, the Bay of Biscay lay extended as far as the horizon, while several of our ships of war were seen sporting upon her bosom. Beneath us lay the pretty little town of St. Jean de Luz, which looked as if it had just been framed out of the Lilliputian scenery of a toy-shop. The town of Bayonne, too, was visible in the distance ; and the view to the right embraced a beautiful well-wooded country, thickly studded with towns and villages, as far as the eye could reach.

Sir Thomas Graham, with the left wing of the army, had, the same morning, passed the Bidassoa, and established them, also, within the French boundary. A brigade of Spaniards, on our right, had made a simultaneous attack on La Rhune, the highest mountain on this part of the Pyrenees, and which, since our last advance, was properly now a part of our position. The enemy, however, refused to quit it; and the firing between them did not cease until long after dark.

The affair in which we were engaged terminated, properly speaking, when we had expelled the enemy from the mountain; but some of our straggling skirmishers contined to follow the retiring foe into the valley beyond, with a view, no doubt, of seeing what a French house contained.

Lord Wellington, preparatory to this movement, had issued an order requiring that private property, of every kind, should be strictly respected; but we had been so long at war with France, that our men had been accustomed to look upon them as their natural enemies, and could not, at first, divest themselves of the idea that they had not a right to partake of the good things abounding about the cottage-doors. Our commandant, however, was determined to see the order rigidly enforced, and it was, therefore, highly amusing to watch the return of the depredators. The first who made his appearance was a bugler, carrying a goose, which, after he had been well beaten about the head with it, was transferred to the provost-marshal. The next was a soldier, with a calf; the soldier was immediately sent to the quarter-guard, and the calf to the provost-marshal. He was followed by another soldier, mounted on a horse, who were, also, both consigned to the same keeping; but, on the soldier stating that he had only got the horse in charge from a volunteer, who was at that time attached to the regiment, he was set at liberty. Presently the volunteer himself came up, and, not observing the colonel lying on the grass, called out among the soldiers, " Who is the —— rascal that sent my horse to the provost-marshal?" " It was I!" said the colonel, to the utter confusion of the querist. Our chief was a good deal nettled at these irregularities; and, some time after, on going to his tent, which was pitched between the roofless walls of a house, conceive his astonishment at finding the calf and the goose hanging in his own larder! He looked serious for a moment, but, on receiving an explanation, and after the row he had made about them, the thing was too ridiculous, and he burst out laughing. It is due to all concerned to state that they had, at last, been honestly come by, for I, as one of his messmates, had purchased the goose from the proper quarter, and another had done the same by the calf.

Not anticipating this day's fight, I had given my pay-serjeant twenty-five guineas, the day before, to distribute among the company; and I did not discover, until too late, that he had neglected to do it, as he disappeared in the course of the action, and was never afterwards heard of. If he was killed, or taken prisoner, he must have been a prize to somebody, though he left me a blank.

Among other incidents of the day, one of our men had a son and heir presented to him by his

Portuguese wife, soon after the action. She had been taken in labour while ascending the mountain; but it did not seem to interfere with her proceedings in the least, for she, and her child, and her donkey, came all three screeching into the camp, immediately after, telling the news, as if it had been something very extraordinary, and none of them a bit the worse.

On the morning of the 9th, we turned out, as usual, an hour before daylight. The sound of musketry, to our right, in our own hemisphere, announced that the French and Spaniards had resumed their unfinished argument of last night, relative to the occupation of La Rhune; while, at the same time, " from our throne of clouds," we had an opportunity of contemplating, with some astonishment, the proceedings of the nether world. A French ship of war, considering St. Jean de Luz no longer a free port, had endeavoured, under cover of the night, to steal alongshore to Bayonne; and, when daylight broke, they had an opportunity of seeing that they were not only within sight of their port, but within sight of a British gun-brig, and, if they entertained any doubts as to which of the two was nearest, their minds were quickly relieved, on that point, by finding that they were not within reach of their port, and strictly within reach of the *guns* of the brig, while two British frigates were bearing down with a press of canvass. The Frenchman returned a few broadsides; he was double the size of the one opposed to him, but, conceiving his case to be hopeless, he at length set fire to the ship, and took to his boats. We watched the progress of the flames until she finally blew up, and disappeared in a column of smoke. The boats of our gun-brig were afterwards seen employed in picking up the odds and ends.

Our friends, the Spaniards, I have no doubt, would have been very glad to have got rid of their opponents in the same kind of way, either by their going without the mountain, or by their taking it with them. But the mountain stood, and the French stood, until we began to wish the mountain, the French, and the Spaniards at the devil; for, although we knew that the affair between them was a matter of no consequence whichever way it went, yet it was impossible for us to feel quite at ease, while a fight was going on so near; it was, therefore, a great relief when, in the afternoon, a few companies of our second brigade were sent to their assistance, as the French then retired without firing another shot. Between the French and us there was no humbug, it was either peace or war. The war, on both sides, was conducted on the grand scale, and, by a tacit sort of understanding, we never teazed each other unnecessarily.

The French, after leaving La Rhune, established their advanced post on Petite La Rhune, a mountain that stood as high as most of its neighbours; but, as its name betokens, it was but a child to its gigantic namesake, of which it seemed as if it had, at a former period, formed a part; but, having been shaken off, like a useless *galloche,* it now stood gaping, open-mouthed, at the place it had left, (and which had now become our advanced post,) while the enemy proceeded to furnish its jaws with a set of teeth, or, in other words, to face it with breast-works, &c. a measure which they invariably had recourse to in every new position.

Encamped on the face of La Rhune, we remained a whole month idle spectators of their preparations, and dearly longing for the day that should afford us an opportunity of penetrating into the more hospitable-looking low country beyond them; for the weather had become excessively cold, and our camp stood exposed to the utmost fury of the almost nightly tempest. Oft have I, in the middle of the night, awoke from a sound sleep, and found my tent on the point of disappearing in the air, like a balloon; and, leaving my warm blankets, been obliged to snatch the mallet, and rush out in the midst of a hailstorm, to peg it down. I think that I now see myself looking like one of those gay creatures of the elements who dwelt (as Shakspeare has it) among the rainbows!

By way of contributing to the warmth of my

tent, I dug a hole inside, which I arranged as a fire-place, carrying the smoke underneath the walls, and building a turf-chimney outside. I was not long in proving the experiment, and, finding that it went exceedingly well, I was not a little vain of the invention. However, it came on to rain very hard while I was dining at a neighbouring tent, and, on my return to my own, I found the fire not only extinguished, but a fountain playing from the same place, up to the roof, watering my bed and baggage, and all sides of it, most refreshingly. This showed me, at the expense of my night's repose, that the rain oozed through the thin spongy surface of earth, and, in particular places, rushed down in torrents between the earth and the rock which it covered; and any incision in the former was sure to produce a fountain.

It is very singular that, notwithstanding our exposure to all the severities of the worst of weather, that we had not a single sick man in the battalion while we remained there.

CHAP. XVII.

Battle of the Nivelle, and Defeat of the Enemy. A Bird of Evil Omen. Chateau D'Arcangues. Prudence. An Enemy's Gratitude. Passage of the Nive, and Battles near Bayonne, from 9th to 13th December.

BATTLE OF THE NIVELLE,

November 10th, 1813.

THE fall of Pampeluna having, at length, left our further movements unshackled by an enemy in the rear, preparations were made for an attack on their position, which, though rather too extended, was formidable by nature, and rendered doubly so by art.

Petite La Rhune was allotted to our division, as their first point of attack; and, accordingly,

the 10th being the day fixed, we moved to our
ground at midnight, on the 9th. The abrupt
ridges in the neighbourhood enabled us to lodge
ourselves, unperceived, within half-musket-shot
of their piquets ; and we had left every description of animal behind us in camp, in order that
neither the barking of dogs nor the neighing of
steeds should give indication of our intentions.
Our signal of attack was to be a gun from Sir
John Hope, who had now succeeded Sir Thomas
Graham in the command of the left wing of the
army.

We stood to our arms at dawn of day, which
was soon followed by the signal-gun ; and each
commanding officer, according to previous instructions, led gallantly off to his point of attack.
The French must have been, no doubt, astonished to see such an armed force spring out
of the ground almost under their noses ; but
they were, nevertheless, prepared behind their
entrenchments, and caused us some loss in passing the short space between us ; but the whole
place was carried within the time required to

walk over it; and, in less than half-an-hour from the commencement of the attack, it was in our possession, with all their tents left standing.

Petite La Rhune was more of an outpost than a part of their position, the latter being a chain of stupendous mountains in its rear; so that while our battalion followed their skirmishers into the valley between, the remainder of our division were forming for the attack on the main position, and waiting for the co-operation of the other divisions, the thunder of whose artillery, echoing along the valleys, proclaimed that they were engaged, far and wide, on both sides of us. About midday our division advanced to the grand attack on the most formidable looking part of the whole of the enemy's position, and, much to our surprise, we carried it with more ease and less loss than the outpost in the morning, a circumstance which we could only account for by supposing that it had been defended by the same troops, and that they did not choose to sustain two *hard* beatings on the same day. The attack succeeded at every point; and, in the

N

evening, we had the satisfaction of seeing the left wing of the army marching into St. Jean de Luz.

Towards the end of the action, Colonel Barnard was struck with a musket-ball, which carried him clean off his horse. The enemy, seeing that they had shot an officer of rank, very maliciously kept up a heavy firing on the spot, while we were carrying him under the brow of the hill. The ball having passed through the lungs, he was spitting blood, and, at the moment, had every appearance of being in a dying state but, to our joy and surprise, he, that day month, rode up to the battalion, when it was in action, near Bayonne; and, I need not add, that he was received with three hearty cheers.

A curious fact occurred in our regiment at this period. Prior to the action of the Nivelle, an owl had perched itself on the tent of one of our officers (Lieut. Doyle). This officer was killed in the battle, and the owl was afterwards seen on Capt. Duncan's tent. His brother-officers quizzed him on the subject, by telling him that he was the next on the list; a joke which Capt. D. did not much relish, and it was prophetic, as he soon afterwards fell at Tarbes.

The movements of the two or three days following placed the enemy within their entrenchments at Bayonne, and the head-quarters of our battalion in the Chateau D'Arcangues, with the outposts of the division at the village of Bassasarry and its adjacents.

I now felt myself both in a humour and a place to enjoy an interval of peace and quietness. The country was abundant in every comfort; the chateau was large, well-furnished, and unoccupied, except by a bed-ridden grandmother, and young Arcangues, a gay rattling young fellow, who furnished us with plenty of good wine, (by our paying for the same,) and made one of our mess.

On the 20th of November a strong reconnoitring party of the enemy examined our chain of posts. They remained a considerable time within half-musket-shot of one of our piquets, but we did not fire, and they seemed at last as if they had all gone away. The place where they had stood bounded our view in that direction, as it was a small sand-hill with a mud-cottage at the end of it; after watching the spot intensely for nearly an hour, and none shewing themselves, my curiosity would keep no longer, and, desiring three men to follow, I rode forward to ascertain the fact. When I cleared the end of the cottage, I found myself within three yards of at least a dozen of them, who were seated in a group behind a small hedge, with their arms laid against the wall of the cottage, and a sentry with sloped arms, and his back towards me, listening to their conversation.

My first impulse was to gallop in amongst them, and order them to surrender; but my three men were still twenty or thirty yards behind, and, as my only chance of success was by surprise, I thought the risk of the delay too great, and, reining back my horse, I made a signal to my men to retire, which, from the soil being a deep sand, we were enabled to do without the slightest noise ; but all the while I had my ears pricked up, expecting every instant to find a ball whistling through my body ; however, as none of them afterwards shewed themselves past the end of the cottage, I concluded that they had remained ignorant of my visit.

We had an affair of some kind, once a week, while we remained there ; and as they were generally trifling, and we always found a good dinner and a good bed in the chateau on our return, we considered them rather a relief than otherwise.

The only instance of a want of professional generosity that I ever had occasion to remark was that of a French officer, which occurred on one of these occasions. We were about to push in their out-posts, for some particular purpose, and I was sent with an order for Lieutenant Gardiner of ours, who was on piquet, to attack the post in his front, as soon as he should see a corresponding movement on his flank, which would take place almost immediately. The enemy's sentries were so near, as to be quite at Mr. Gardiner's mercy, who immediately said to me, " Well, I wo'n't kill these unfortunate rascals at all events, but shall tell them to go in and join their piquet." I applauded his motives, and rode off; but I had only gone a short distance when I heard a volley of musketry behind me ; and, seeing that it had come from the French piquet, I turned back to see what had happened, and found that the officer commanding it had no sooner got his sentries so generously restored to him, than he instantly formed his piquet and fired a volley at Lieutenant Gardiner, who was walking a little apart from his men, waiting for the expected signal. The balls all fell near, without touching him, and, for the honour of the French army, I was glad to hear afterwards that the officer alluded to was a militia-man.

BATTLES NEAR BAYONNE.

December 9th, 10th, 11th, 12th, and 13th, 1813.

The centre and left wing of our army ad-

vanced on the morning of the 9th of December,
and drove the enemy within their entrenchments, threatening an attack on their lines.
Lord Wellington had the double object, in this
movement, of reconnoitring their works, and
effecting the passage of the Nive with his right
wing. The rivers Nive and Adour unite in the
town of Bayonne, so that while we were threatening to storm the works on one side, Sir Rowland Hill passed the Nive, without opposition,
on the other, and took up his ground, with his
right on the Adour and his left on the Nive, on
a contracted space, within a very short distance
of the walls of the town. On our side we were
engaged in a continued skirmish until dark,
when we retired to our quarters, under the sup-
position that we had got our usual week's allowance, and that we should remain quiet again for
a time.

We turned out at daylight on the 10th; but,
as there was a thick drizzling rain which
prevented us from seeing any thing, we soon
turned in again. My servant soon after came

to tell me that Sir Lowry Cole, and some of his staff, had just ascended to the top of the chateau, a piece of information which did not quite please me, for I fancied that the general had just discovered our quarter to be better than his own, and had come for the purpose of taking possession of it. However, in less than five minutes, we received an order for our battalion to move up instantly to the support of the piquets; and, on my descending to the door, to mount my horse, I found Sir Lowry standing there, who asked if we had received any orders; and, on my telling him that we had been ordered up to support the piquets, he immediately desired a staff-officer to order up one of his brigades to the rear of the chateau. This was one of the numerous instances in which we had occasion to admire the prudence and forethought of the great Wellington! He had foreseen the attack that would take place, and had his different divisions disposed to meet it. We no sooner moved up, than we found ourselves a party engaged along with the

piquets; and, under a heavy skirmishing fire,
retiring gradually from hedge to hedge, according as the superior force of the enemy compelled
us to give ground, until we finally retired within
our home, the chateau, which was the first part
of our position that was meant to be defended in
earnest. We had previously thrown up a mud
rampart around it, and loop-holed the different
out-houses, so that we had nothing now to do,
but to line the walls and shew determined fight.
The forty-third occupied the church-yard to our
left, which was also partially fortified; and the
third Cácadores and our third battalion, occupied
the space between, behind the hedge-rows, while
the fourth division was in readiness to support
us from the rear. The enemy came up to the
opposite ridge, in formidable numbers, and
began blazing at our windows and loop-holes,
and shewing some disposition to attempt it by
storm; but they thought better of it and withdrew their columns a short distance to the rear,
leaving the nearest hedge lined with their skirmishers. An officer of ours, Mr. Hopewood, and

one of our serjeants, had been killed in the field
opposite, within twenty yards of where the enemy's skirmishers now were. We were very
anxious to get possession of their bodies, but
had not force enough to effect it. Several
French soldiers came through the hedge, at different times, with the intention, as we thought,
of plundering, but our men shot every one who
attempted to go near them, until towards
evening, when a French officer approached,
waving a white handkerchief and pointing
to some of his men who were following him
with shovels. Seeing that his intention was to
bury them, we instantly ceased firing, nor did
we renew it again that night.

The forty-third, from their post at the church,
kept up an incessant shower of musketry the
whole of the day, at what was conceived, at the
time, to be a very long range; but from the
quantity of balls which were afterwards found
sticking in every tree, where the enemy stood,
it was evident that their birth must have been
rather uncomfortable.

One of our officers, in the course of the day, had been passing through a deep road-way, between two banks, with hedge-rows, when, to his astonishment, a dragoon and his horse tumbled heels over head into the road, as if they had been fired out of a cloud. Neither of them were the least hurt; but it must have been no joke that tempted him to take such a flight.

Soult expected, by bringing his whole force to bear on our centre and left wing, that he would have succeeded in forcing it, or, at all events, of obliging Lord Wellington to withdraw Sir Rowland Hill from beyond the Nive; but he effected neither, and darkness left the two armies on the ground which they had fought on.

General Alten and Sir James Kempt took up their quarters with us in the chateau: our sentries and those of the enemy stood within pistol-shot of each other in the ravine below.

Young Arcangues, I presume, must have been rather disappointed at the result of the day; for, even giving him credit for every kindly feeling towards us, his wishes must still have been in favour of his countrymen; but when he found that his chateau was to be a bone of contention, it then became his interest that we should keep possession of it; and he held out every inducement for us to do so; which, by the by, was quite unnecessary, seeing that our own comfort so much depended on it. However, though his supplies of claret had failed some days before, he now discovered some fresh cases in the cellar, which he immediately placed at our disposal; and, that our dire resolve to defend the fortress should not be melted by weak woman's wailings, he fixed an arm-chair on a mule, mounted his grandmother on it, and sent her off to the rear, while the balls were whizzing about the neighbourhood in a manner to which even she, poor old lady, was not altogether insensible, though she had become a mounted heroine at a period when she had given up all idea of ever sitting on any thing more lively than a coffin.

During the whole of the 11th each army retained the same ground, and though there was an occasional exchange of shots at different points, yet nothing matérial occurred.

The enemy began throwing up a six-gun battery opposite our chateau; and we employed ourselves in strengthening the works, as a precautionary measure, though we had not much to dread from it, as they were so strictly within range of our rifles, that he must have been a lucky artilleryman who stood there to fire a second shot.

In the course of the night a brigade of Belgians, who were with the French army, having heard that their country had declared for their legitimate king, passed over to our side, and surrendered.

On the 12th there was heavy firing and hard fighting, all day, to our left, but we remained perfectly quiet. Towards the afternoon, Sir James Kempt formed our brigade, for the purpose of expelling the enemy from the hill next the chateau, to which he thought them rather too near; but, just as we reached our different points for commencing the attack, we were recalled, and nothing further occurred.

I went, about one o'clock in the morning, to visit our different piquets; and seeing an unusual number of fires in the enemy's lines, I concluded that they had lit them to mask some movement; and taking a patrole with me, I stole cautiously forward, and found that they had left the ground altogether. I immediately returned, and reported the circumstance to General Alten, who sent off a despatch to apprize Lord Wellington.

As soon as day began to dawn, on the morning of the 13th, a tremendous fire of artillery and musketry was heard to our right. Soult had withdrawn every thing from our front in the course of the night, and had now attacked Sir Rowland Hill with his whole force. Lord Wellington, in expectation of this attack, had, last night, reinforced Sir Rowland Hill with the sixth division; which enabled him to occupy his contracted position so strongly, that Soult, unable to bring more than his own front to bear upon him, sustained a signal and sanguinary defeat.

Lord Wellington galloped into the yard of our chateau, soon after the attack had commenced, and demanded, with his usual quickness, what was to be seen? Sir James Kempt, who was spying at the action from an upper window, told him; and, after desiring Sir James to order Sir Lowry Cole to follow him with the fourth division, he galloped off to the scene of action. In the afternoon, when all was over, he called in again, on his return to head-quarters, and told us, " that it was the most glorious affair that he " had ever seen; and that the enemy had abso-" lutely left upwards of five thousand men, killed " and wounded, on the ground."

This was the last action in which we were concerned, near Bayonne. The enemy seemed quite satisfied with what they had got; and offered us no further molestation, but withdrew within their works.

CHAP. XVIII.

TOWARDS the end of the month, some divisions
of the French army having left Bayonne, and
ascended the right bank of the Adour, it produced a corresponding movement on our side,
by which our division then occupied Ustaritz,
and some neighbouring villages; a change of
quarters we had no reason to rejoice in.

At Arcangues, notwithstanding the influence
of our messmate, " the Seigneur du Village,"
our table had, latterly, exhibited gradual symp-

toms of decay. But *here,* our voracious predecessors had not only swallowed the calf, but the
cow, and, literally, left us nothing ; so that,
from an occasional turkey, or a pork-pie, we
were now, all at once, reduced to our daily ration
of a withered pound of beef. A great many
necessaries of life could certainly be procured
from St. Jean de Luz, but the prices there were
absolutely suicidical. The suttlers' shops were
too small to hold both their goods and their
consciences ; so that, every pin's worth they sold
cost us a dollar; and as every dollar cost us
seven shillings, they were, of course, not so
plenty as bad dinners. I have often regretted
that the enemy never got an opportunity of
having the run of their shops for a few minutes,
that they might have been, in some measure,
punished for their sins, even in this world.

The house that held our table, too, was but a
wretched apology for the one we had left. A
bitter wind continued to blow; and as the
granary of a room which we occupied, on the
first floor, had no fire-place, we immediately

proceeded to provide it with one, and continued filling it up with such a load of bricks and mortar that the first floor was on the point of becoming the ground one; and, having only a choice of evils, on such an emergency, we, as usual, adopted that which appeared to us to be the least, cutting down the only two fruit-trees in the garden to prop it up with. We were rather on doubtful terms with the landlord before, but this put us all square—no terms at all.

Our animals, too, were in a woful plight, for want of forage. We were obliged to send our baggage ones, every week, for their rations of corn, three days' march, through oceans of mud, which ought, properly, to have been navigated with boats. The whole cavalcade always moved under the charge of an officer, and many were the anxious looks that we took with our spy-glasses, from a hill overlooking the road, on the days of their expected return, each endeavouring to descry his own. Mine came back to me twice; but " the pitcher that goes often to the well" was verified in his third trip, for—he perished in a muddy grave.

His death, however, was not so unexpected as it might have been, for, although I cannot literally say that he had been dying by inches, seeing that he had walked all the way from the frontiers of Portugal, yet he had, nevertheless, been doing it on the grand scale—by miles. I only fell in with him the day before the commencement of the campaign, and, after reconnoitring him with my usual judgement, and seeing that he was in possession of the regulated quantity of eyes, legs, and mouth, and concluding that they were all calculated to perform their different functions, I took him, as a man does his wife, for better and for worse; and it was not until the end of the first day's march that I found he had a broken jaw-bone, and could not eat, and I had, therefore, been obliged to support him all along on spoon diet; he was a capital horse, only for that!

It has already been written, in another man's book, that we always require just a little more than we have got to make us perfectly happy; and, as we had given this neighbourhood a fair trial, and *that little* was not to be found in it, we were very glad when, towards the end of February, we were permitted to look for it a little further on. We broke up from quarters on the 21st, leaving Sir John Hope, with the left wing of the army, in the investment of Bayonne, Lord Wellington followed Soult with the remainder.

The new clothing for the different regiments of the army had, in the mean time, been gradually arriving at St. Jean de Luz; and, as the commissariat transport was required for other purposes, not to mention that a man's new coat always looks better on his own back than it does on a mule's, the different regiments marched there for it in succession. It did not come to our turn until we had taken a stride to the front, as far as La Bastide; our retrograde movement, therefore, obliged us to bid adieu to our division for some time.

On our arrival at St. Jean de Luz, we found our new clothing, and some new friends in the

family of our old friend, Arcangues, which was
one of the most respectable in the district, and
who showed us a great deal of kindness. As it
happened to be the commencement of Lent, the
young ladies were, at first, doubtful as to the
propriety of joining us in any of the gaieties;
but, after a short consultation, they arranged
it with their consciences, and joined in the waltz
right merrily. Mademoiselle was really an exceedingly nice girl, and the most lively companion in arms (in a waltz) that I ever met.

Our clothing detained us there two days;
on the third, we proceeded to rejoin the division.

The pride of ancestry is very tenaciously up-
held among the Basques, who are the moun-
taineers of that district. I had a fancy that
most of them grew wild, like their trees, without
either fathers or mothers, and was, therefore,
much amused, one day, to hear a fellow, with a
Tam O'Shanter's bonnet, and a pair of bare
legs, tracing his descent from the first man,
and maintaining that he spoke the same lan-

guage too. He might have added, if further proof were wanting, that he, also, wore the same kind of shoes and stockings.

On the 27th February, 1814, we marched, all day, to the tune of a cannonade; it was the battle of Orthes; and, on our arrival, in the evening, at the little town of St. Palais, we were very much annoyed to find the seventy-ninth regiment stationed there, who handed us a general order, desiring that the last-arrived regiment should relieve the preceding one in charge of the place. This was the more vexatious, knowing that there was no other regiment behind to relieve us. It was a nice little town, and we were treated, by the inhabitants, like friends and allies, experiencing much kindness and hospitality from them; but a rifleman, in the rear, is like a fish out of the water; he feels that he is not in his place. Seeing no other mode of obtaining a release, we, at length, began detaining the different detachments who were proceeding to join their regiments, with a view of forming a battalion of them; but, by the time that we had collected a sufficient number for that purpose, we received an order, from head-quarters, to join the army; when, after a few days' forced marches, we had, at length, the happiness of overtaking our division a short distance beyond the town of Aire. The battle of Orthes was the only affair of consequence that had taken place during our absence.

We remained stationary, near Aire, until the middle of March, when the army was again put in motion.

On the morning of the 19th, while we were marching along the road, near the town of Tarbes, we saw what appeared to be a small piquet of the enemy, on the top of a hill to our left, looking down upon us, when a company of our second battalion was immediately sent to dislodge them. The enemy, however, increased in number, in proportion to those sent against them, until not only the whole of the second, but our own, and the third battalion were eventually brought into action; and still we had more than double our number opposed to us;

but we, nevertheless, drove them from the field with great slaughter, after a desperate struggle of a few minutes, in which we had eleven officers killed and wounded. As this fight was purely a rifle one, and took place within sight of the whole army, I may be justified in giving the following quotation from the author of " Twelve Years' Military Adventure," who was a spectator, and who, in allusion to this affair, says, " Our rifles were immediately sent to dislodge " the French from the hills on our left, and our " battalion was ordered to support them. No- " thing could exceed the manner in which the " ninety-fifth set about the business........ " Certainly I never saw such skirmishers as the " ninety-fifth, now the rifle brigade. They could " do the work much better and with infinitely " less loss than any other of our best light " troops. They possessed an individual bold- " ness, a mutual understanding, and a quickness " of eye, in taking advantage of the ground, " which, taken altogether, I never saw equalled. " They were, in fact, as much superior to the

" French *voltiguers*, as the latter were to our
" skirmishers in general. As our regiment was
" often employed in supporting them, I think I
" am fairly qualified to speak of their merits."

We followed the enemy until dark, when, after
having taken up our ground and lit our fires,
they rather maliciously opened a cannonade
upon us; but, as few of their shots took effect,
we did not put ourselves to the inconvenience of
moving, and they soon desisted.

We continued in pursuit daily, until we finally
arrived on the banks of the Garonne, opposite
Toulouse. The day after our arrival an attempt was made, by our engineers, to throw
a bridge across the river, above the town;
and we had assembled one morning, to be in
readiness to pass over, but they were obliged
to abandon it for want of the necessary number of pontoons, and we returned again to
quarters.

We were stationed, for several days, in the
suburb of St. Ciprien, where we found ourselves
exceedingly comfortable. It consisted chiefly of

o

the citizens' country houses, and an abundance
of the public tea and fruit accommodations, with
which every large city is surrounded, for the
temptation of Sunday parties ; and, as the inhabitants had all fled hurriedly into town, leaving
their cellars, generally speaking, well stocked
with a tolerable kind of wine, we made ourselves
at home.

It was finally determined that the passage of
the river should be tried below the town, and,
preparatory thereto, we took ground to our left,
and got lodged in the chateau of a rich old
West-India-man. He was a tall ramrod of a
fellow, upwards of six feet high, withered to a
cinder, and had a pair of green eyes, which
looked as if they belonged to somebody else,
who was looking through his eye-holes ; but,
despite his imperfections, he had got a young
wife, and she was nursing a young child. The
" Green Man" (as we christened him) was not,
however, so bad as he looked ; and we found our
billet such a good one, that when we were called
away to fight, after a few days' residence with

him, I question, if left to our choice, whether we would not have rather remained where we were!

A bridge having, at length, been established, about a league below the town, two British divisions passed over; but the enemy, by floating timber and other things down the stream, succeeded in carrying one or two of the pontoons from their moorings, which prevented any more from crossing either that day or the succeeding one. It was expected that the French would have taken advantage of this circumstance, to attack the two divisions on the other side; but they thought it more prudent to wait the attack in their own strong hold, and in doing so I believe they acted wisely, for these two divisions had both flanks secured by the river, their position was not too extended for their numbers, and they had a clear space in their front, which was flanked by artillery from the commanding ground on our side of the river; so that, altogether, they would have been found ugly customers to any body who chose to meddle with them.

The bridge was re-established on the night of the 9th, and, at daylight next morning, we bade adieu to the *Green Man*, inviting him to come and see us in Toulouse in the evening. He laughed at the idea, telling us that we should be lucky fellows if ever we got in; and, at all events, he said, that he would bet a *déjeúné à la forchette* for a dozen, that we did not enter it in three days from that time. I took the bet, and won, but the old rogue never came to pay me.

We crossed the river, and advanced sufficiently near to the enemy's position to be just out of the reach of their fire, where we waited until dispositions were made for the attack, which took place as follows:—

Sir Rowland Hill, who remained on the left bank of the Garonne, made a show of attacking the bridge and suburb of the town on that side.

On our side of the river the Spanish army, which had never hitherto taken an active part in any of our general actions, now claimed the post of honour, and advanced to storm the strongest part of the heights. Our division was ordered to support them in the low grounds, and, at the same time, to threaten a point of the canal; and Picton, who was on our right, was ordered to make a false attack on the canal. These were all that were visible to us. The remaining divisions of the army were in continuation to the left.

The Spaniards, anxious to monopolize all the glory, I rather think, moved on to the attack a little too soon, and before the British divisions on their left were in readiness to co-operate; however, be that as it may, they were soon in a blaze of fire, and began walking through it, at first, with a great show of gallantry and determination; but their courage was not altogether screwed up to the sticking point, and the nearer they came to the critical pass, the less prepared they seemed to meet it, until they all finally faced to the right-about, and came back upon us as fast as their heels could carry them, pursued by the enemy.

We instantly advanced to their relief, and
concluded that they would have rallied behind
us; but they had no idea of doing any thing
of the kind; for, when with *Cuesta* and some
of the other Spanish generals, they had been
accustomed, under such circumstances, to run a
hundred miles at a time; so that, passing through
the intervals of our division, they went clear off
to the rear, and we never saw them more. The
moment the French found us interpose between
them and the Spaniards they retired within
their works.

The only remark that Lord Wellington was
said to have made on their conduct, after waiting to see whether they would stand after they
got out of the reach of the enemy's shot, was,
" well, d—— me, if ever I saw ten thousand
men run a race before!" However, notwithstanding their disaster, many of their officers
certainly evinced great bravery, and on their
account it is to be regretted that the attack
was made so soon, for they would otherwise

have carried their point with little loss, either of life or credit, as the British divisions on the left soon after stormed and carried all the other works, and obliged those who had been opposed to the Spaniards to evacuate theirs without firing another shot.

When the enemy were driven from the heights, they retired within the town, and the canal then became their line of defence, which they maintained the whole of the next day; but in the course of the following night they left the town altogether, and we took possession of it on the morning of the 12th.

The inhabitants of Toulouse hoisted the white flag, and declared for the Bourbons the moment that the French army had left it; and, in the course of the same day, Colonel Cooke arrived from Paris, with the extraordinary news of Napoleon's abdication. Soult has been accused of having been in possession of that fact prior to the battle of Toulouse; but, to disprove such an assertion, it can only be necessary to think, for a moment, whether he would not have made it public the day after the battle, while he yet held possession of the town, as it would not only have enabled him to keep it, but, to those who knew no better, it might have given him a shadow of claim to the victory, if he chose to avail himself of it; and I have known a victory claimed by a French marshal on more slender grounds. In place of knowing it then, he did not even believe it now; and we were absolutely obliged to follow him a day's march beyond Toulouse before he agreed to an armistice.

The news of the peace, at this period, certainly sounded as strangely in our ears as it did in those of the French marshal, for it was a change that we never had contemplated. We had been born in war, reared in war, and war was our trade; and what soldiers had to do in peace, was a problem yet to be solved among us.

After remaining a few days at Toulouse, we were sent into quarters, in the town of Castle-

Sarazin, along with our old companions in arms, the fifty-second, to wait the necessary arrangements for our final removal from France.

Castle-Sarazin is a respectable little town, on the right bank of the Garonne; and its inhabitants received us so kindly, that every officer found in his quarter a family home. We there, too, found both the time and the opportunity of exercising one of the agreeable professions to which we had long been strangers, that of making love to the pretty little girls with which the place abounded ; when, after a three months' residence among them, the fatal order arrived for our march to Bordeaux, for embarkation, the buckets full of salt tears that were shed by men who had almost forgotten the way to weep was quite ridiculous. I have never yet, however, clearly made out whether people are most in love when they are laughing or when they are crying. Our greatest love writers certainly give the preference to the latter. *Scott* thinks that " love is loveliest when it's bathed in tears ;" and *Moore* tells his mistress to " give smiles to those who love her less, but to keep her tears for him;" but what pleasure he can take in seeing her in affliction, I cannot make out; nor, for the soul of me, can I see why a face full of smiles should not be every bit as valuable as one of tears, seeing that it is so much more pleasant to look at.

I have rather wandered, in search of an apology for my own countenance not having gone into mourning on that melancholy occasion; for, to tell the truth, (and if I had a visage sensible to such an impression, I should blush while I tell it,) I was as much in love as any body, up nearly to the last moment, when I fell out of it, as it were, by a miracle; but, probably, a history of love's last look may be considered as my justification. The day before our departure, in returning from a ride, I overtook my love and her sister, strolling by the river's side, and, instantly dismounting, I joined in their walk. My horse was following, at the length of his bridle-reins, and, while I was engaged in conversation with the sister, the other dropped behind, and, when I looked round, I found her mounted *astride* on my horse! and with such a pair of legs, too! It was rather too good; and " Richard was himself again."

Although released, under the foregoing circumstances, from individual attachment, that of a general nature continued strong as ever; and, without an exception on either side, I do believe, that we parted with mutual regret, and with the most unbounded love and good feeling towards each other. We exchanged substantial proofs of it while together; we continued to do so after we had parted; nor were we forgotten when we were *no more!* It having appeared, in some of the newspapers, a year afterwards, that every one of our officers had been killed at Waterloo, that the regiment had been brought out of the action by a volunteer, and the report having come to the knowledge of our Castel-Sarazin friends, they drew up a letter, which they sent to our commanding officer, signed by every person of respectability in the place, lamenting our fate, expressing a hope that the report might have been exaggerated, and entreating to be informed as to the particular fate of each individual officer, whom they mentioned by name. They were kind good-hearted souls, and may God bless them!

CHAP. XIX.

Commencement of the War of 1815. Embark for Rotterdam. Ship's Stock. Ship struck. A Pilot, a Smuggler, and a Lawyer. A Boat without Stock. Join the Regiment at Brussels.

I HAVE endeavoured, in this book of mine, to measure out the peace and war in due proportions, according to the spirit of the times it speaks of; and, as there appears to me to be as much peace in the last chapter as occurred in Europe between 1814 and 1815, I shall, with the reader's permission, lodge my regiment, at once, on Dover-heights, and myself in Scotland, taking a shot at the last of the woodcocks, which happened to be our relative positions, when Bonaparte's escape from Elba once more summoned the army to the field.

The first intimation I had of it was by a letter, informing me of the embarkation of the battalion for the Netherlands, and desiring me to join them there, without delay; and, finding that a brig was to sail, the following day, from Leith to Rotterdam, I took a passage on board of her. She was an odd one to look at, but the captain assured me that she was a good one to go; and, besides, that he had provided every thing that was elegant for our entertainment. The latter piece of information I did not think of questioning until too late to profit by it, for I had the mortification to discover, the first day, that his whole stock consisted in a quarter of lamb, in addition to the ship's own, with a few cabbages, and five gallons of whiskey.

After having been ten days at sea, I was awoke, one morning before daylight, with the ship's grinding over a sand-bank, on the coast of Holland; fortunately, it did not blow hard, and a pilot soon after came alongside, who, after exacting a reward suitable to the occasion, at length, consented to come on board, and extricated us from our perilous situation, carrying the vessel into the entrance of one of the small branches of the river leading up to Rotterdam, where we came to anchor. The captain was very desirous of appealing to a magistrate for a reduction in the exorbitant demand of the pilot; and I accompanied him on shore for that purpose. An Englishman made up to us at the landing-place, and said that his name was C——, that he had made his fortune by smuggling, and, though he was not permitted to spend it in his native country, that he had the greatest pleasure in being of service to his countrymen. As this was exactly the sort of person we were in search of, the Captain explained his grievance; and the other said that he would conduct him to a gentleman who would soon put that to rights. We, accordingly, walked to the adjoining village, in one of the houses of which he introduced us, formally, to a tall Dutchman, with a pipe in his mouth and a pen behind his ear, who, after hearing the story, proceeded to commit it, in large characters, to a quire of foolscap.

The cautious nature of the Scotchman did not altogether like the appearance of the man of business, and demanding, through the interpreter, whether there would be any thing to pay for his proceedings? he was told that it would cost five guineas. " Five devils," said Saunders ; " What is it for ?" " For a protest," said the other. " D—n the protest," said the captain ; " I came here to save five guineas, and not to pay five more." I could stand the scene no longer, and rushed out of the house, under the pretence of seeing the village ; and on my return to the ship, half an hour afterwards, I found the captain fast asleep. I know not whether he swallowed the remainder of the five gallons of whiskey, in addition to his five-guinea grievance, but I could not shake him out of it, although the mate and I tried, alternately, for upwards of two hours ; and indeed I never heard whether he ever got out of it,—for when

I found that they had to go outside to find another passage up to Rotterdam, I did not think it prudent to trust myself any longer in the hands of such artists, and, taking leave of the sleeper, with a last ineffectual shake, I hired a boat to take me through the passage in which we then were.

We started with a stiff fair wind, and the boatman assured me that we should reach Rotterdam in less than five hours (forty miles); but it soon lulled to a dead calm, which left us to the tedious operation of tiding it up; and, to mend the matter, we had not a fraction of money between us, nor any thing to eat or drink. I bore starvation all that day and night, with the most christian-like fortitude; but, the next morning, I could stand it no longer, and sending the boatman on shore, to a neighbouring house, I instructed him either to beg or steal something, whichever he should find the most prolific; but he was a clumsy hand at both, and came on board again with only a very small quantity of coffee. It, however, afforded some relief, and in the afternoon we reached the town of Dort, and, on lodging my baggage in pawn with a French inn-keeper, he advanced me the means of going on to Rotterdam, where I got cash for the bill which I had on a merchant there. Once more furnished with the " sinews of war," with my feet on *terra firma,* I lost no time in setting forward to Antwerp, and from thence to Brussels, when I had the happiness of rejoining my battalion, which was then quartered in the city.

Brussels was, at this time, a scene of extraordinary preparation, from the succession of troops who were hourly arriving, and in their formation into brigades and divisions. We had the good fortune to be attached to the brigade of our old and favourite commander, Sir James Kempt, and in the fifth division, under Sir Thomas Picton. It was the only division quartered in Brussels, the others being all towards the French frontier, except the Duke of Brunswick's corps, which lay on the Antwerp road.

CHAP. XX.

Relative Situation of the Troops.   March from Brussels.
The Prince and the Beggar.   Battle of Quatre-Bras.

As our division was composed of crack regiments, under crack commanders, and headed by
fire-eating generals, we had little to do the first
fortnight after my arrival, beyond indulging in
all the amusements of our delightful quarter;
but, as the middle of June approached, we began
to get a little more on the *qui vive*, for we were
aware that Napoleon was about to make a
dash at some particular point; and, as he was
not the sort of general to give his opponent
an idea of the when and the where, the greater
part of our army was necessarily disposed
along the frontier, to meet him at his own

place. They were of course too much extended
to offer effectual resistance in their advanced
position; but as our division and the Duke of
Brunswick's corps were held in reserve, at
Brussels, in readiness to be thrust at whatever
point might be attacked, they were a sufficient
additional force to check the enemy for the time
required to concentrate the army.

On the 14th of June it was generally known,
among the military circles in Brussels, that
Buonaparte was in motion, at the head of his
troops; and though his movement was understood
to point at the Prussians, yet he was not sufficiently advanced to afford a correct clue to his
intentions.

We were, the whole of the 15th, on the most
anxious look out for news from the front; but no
report had been received prior to the hour of
dinner. I went, about seven in the evening, to
take a stroll in the park, and meeting one of the
Duke's staff, he asked me, *en passant*, whether
my pack-saddles were all ready? I told him

that they were nearly so, and added, " I sup-
" pose they wo'n't be wanted, at all events,
" before to-morrow ?" to which he replied, in
the act of leaving me, " If you have any pre-
" paration to make, I would recommend you
" not to delay so long," I took the hint, and
returning to quarters, remained in momentary
expectation of an order to move. The bugles
sounded to arms about two hours after.

To the credit of our battalion, be it recorded,
that, although the greater part were in bed when
the assembly sounded, and billetted over the
most distant parts of that extensive city, every
man was on his alarm-post before eleven o'clock,
in a complete state of marching order : whereas,
it was nearly two o'clock in the morning before
we were joined by the others.

As a grand ball was to take place the same
night, at the Duchess of Richmond's, the order
for the assembling of the troops was accompanied
by permission for any officer who chose to remain for the ball, provided that he joined his

regiment early in the morning. Several of ours took advantage of it.

Brussels was, at that time, thronged with British temporary residents; who, no doubt, in the course of the two last days, must have heard, through their military acquaintance, of the immediate prospect of hostilities. But, accustomed, on their own ground, to hear of those things as a piece of news in which they were not personally concerned; and never dreaming of danger, in streets crowded with the gay uniforms of their countrymen; it was not until their defenders were summoned to the field, that they were fully sensible of their changed circumstances; and the suddenness of the danger multiplying its horrors, many of them were now seen running about in the wildest state of distraction.

Waiting for the arrival of the other regiments, we endeavoured to snatch an hour's repose on the pavement; but we were every instant disturbed, by ladies as well as gentlemen; some stumbling over us in the dark—some shaking us out of our sleep, to be told the news—and not a few, conceiving their immediate safety depending upon our standing in place of lying. All those who applied for the benefit of my advice, I recommended to go home to bed, to keep themselves perfectly cool, and to rest assured that, if their departure from the city became necessary, (which I very much doubted,) they would have at least one whole day to prepare for it, as we were leaving some beef and potatoes behind us, for which, I was sure, we would fight, rather than abandon!

The whole of the division having, at length, assembled, we were put in motion about three o'clock on the morning of the 16th, and advanced to the village of Waterloo, where, forming in a field adjoining the road, our men were allowed to prepare their breakfasts. I succeeded in getting mine, in a small inn, on the left hand side of the village.

Lord Wellington joined us about nine o'clock ; and, from his very particular orders, to see that the roads were kept clear of baggage, and every thing likely to impede the movements of the troops, I have since been convinced that his lordship had thought it probable that the position of Waterloo might, even that day, have become the scene of action; for it was a good broad road, on which there were neither the quantity of baggage nor of troops moving at the time, to excite the slightest apprehension of confusion. Leaving us halted, he galloped on to the front, followed by his staff; and we were soon after joined by the Duke of Brunswick, with his corps of the army.

His highness dismounted near the place where I was standing, and seated himself on the roadside, along with his adjutant-general. He soon after despatched his companion on some duty; and I was much amused to see the vacated place immediately filled by an old beggar-man; who, seeing nothing in the black hussar uniform beside him denoting the high rank of the wearer, began to grunt and scratch himself most luxuriously! The duke shewed a degree of

courage which few would, under such circumstances; for he maintained his post until the
return of his officer, when he very jocularly said,
" Well, O——n, you see that your place was
" not long unoccupied!"—How little idea had I,
at the time, that the life of the illustrious
speaker was limited to three short hours!

About twelve o'clock an order arrived for the
troops to advance, leaving their baggage behind;
and though it sounded warlike, yet we did
not expect to come in contact with the enemy,
at all events, on *that* day. But, as we moved
forward, the symptoms of their immediate presence kept gradually increasing; for we presently
met a cart-load of wounded Belgians; and, after
passing through Genappe, the distant sound of
a solitary gun struck on the listening ear. But
all doubt on the subject was quickly removed;
for, on ascending the rising ground, where
stands the village of Quatre Bras, we saw
a considerable plain in our front, flanked on
each side by a wood; and on another acclivity

P

beyond, we could perceive the enemy descending towards us, in most imposing numbers.

Quatre Bras, at that time, consisted of only three or four houses; and, as its name betokens, I believe, stood at the junction of four roads; on one of which we were moving; a second, inclined to the right; a third, in the same degree, to the left; and the fourth, I conclude, must have gone backwards; but, as I had not an eye in that direction, I did not see it.

The village was occupied by some Belgians, under the Prince of Orange, who had an advanced post in a large farm-house, at the foot of the road, which inclined to the right; and a part of his division, also, occupied the wood on the same side.

Lord Wellington, I believe, after leaving us at Waterloo, galloped on to the Prussian position at Ligny, where he had an interview with Blucher, in which they concerted measures for their mutual co-operation. When we arrived at Quatre Bras, however, we found him in a field near the Belgian out-post; and the enemy's guns were just beginning to play upon the spot where he stood, surrounded by a numerous staff.

We halted for a moment on the brow of the hill; and as Sir Andrew Barnard galloped forward to the head-quarter group; I followed, to be in readiness to convey any orders to the battalion. The moment we approached, Lord Fitzroy Somerset, separating himself from the duke, said, " Barnard, you are wanted instantly; " take your battalion and endeavour to get pos- " session of that village," pointing to one on the face of the rising ground, down which the enemy were moving ; " but if you cannot do " that, secure that wood on the left, and keep " the road open for communication with the " Prussians." We instantly moved in the given direction; but, ere we had got half-way to the village, we had the mortification to see the enemy throw such a force into it, as rendered any attempt to retake it, with our numbers, utterly hopeless ; and as another strong body of them were hastening towards the wood, which was the second object pointed out to us, we immediately brought them to action, and secured it. In moving to that point, one of our men went raving mad, from excessive heat. The poor fellow cut a few extraordinary capers, and died in the course of a few minutes.

While our battalion-reserve occupied the front of the wood, our skirmishers lined the side of the road, which was the Prussian line of communication. The road itself, however, was crossed by such a shower of balls, that none but a desperate traveller would have undertaken a journey on it. We were presently reinforced by a small battalion of foreign light troops, with whose assistance we were in hopes to have driven the enemy a little further from it; but they were a raw body of men, who had never before been under fire; and, as they could not be prevailed upon to join our skirmishers, we could make no use of them whatever. Their conduct, in fact, was an exact representation of Mathews's ludicrous one of the American militia, for Sir Andrew Barnard repeatedly pointed out to them

which was the French, and which our side;
and, after explaining that they were not to fire
a shot until they joined our skirmishers, the
word " March!" was given; but *march*, to
them, was always the signal to fire, for they
stood fast, and began blazing away, chiefly at
our skirmishers too; the officers commanding
whom were every time sending back to say
that we were shooting them; until we were, at
last, obliged to be satisfied with whatever advantages their appearance could give, as even
that was of some consequence, where troops
were so scarce.

Buonaparte's attack on the Prussians had already commenced, and the fire of artillery and
musketry, in that direction, was tremendous;
but the intervening higher ground prevented us
from seeing any part of it.

The plain to our right, which we had just
quitted, had, likewise, become the scene of a
sanguinary and unequal contest. Our division,
after we left it, deployed into line, and, in advancing, met and routed the French infantry;

but, in following up their advantage, they encountered a furious charge of cavalry, and were
obliged to throw themselves into squares to receive it. With the exception of one regiment,
however, which had two companies cut to
pieces, they were not only successful in resisting
the attack, but made awful havock in the
enemy's ranks, who, nevertheless, continued
their forward career, and went sweeping past
them, like a whirlwind, up to the village of
Quatre Bras, to the confusion and consternation
of the numerous useless appendages of our army,
who were there assembled, waiting the result of
the battle.

The forward movement of the enemy's cavalry
gave their infantry time to rally; and, strongly
reinforced with fresh troops, they again advanced to the attack. This was a crisis in
which, according to Buonaparte's theory, the
victory was theirs, by all the rules of war, for
they held superior numbers, both before and
behind us; but the gallant old Picton, who had
been trained in a different school, did not choose

to confine himself to rules in those matters; despising the force in his rear, he advanced, charged, and routed those in his front, which created such a panic among the others, that they galloped back through the intervals in his division, with no other object in view but their own safety. After this desperate conflict, the firing, on both sides, lulled almost to a calm for nearly an hour, while each was busy in renewing their order of battle. The Duke of Bruuswick had been killed early in the action, endeavouring to rally his young troops, who were unable to withstand the impetuosity of the French; and, as we had no other cavalry force in the field, the few British infantry regiments present, having to bear the full brunt of the enemy's superior force of both arms, were now considerably reduced in numbers.

The battle, on the side of the Prussians, still continued to rage in an unceasing roar of artillery. About four, in the afternoon, a troop of their dragoons came, as a patrole, to inquire how it fared with us, and told us, in passing, that they still maintained their position. Their day, however, was still to be decided, and, indeed, for that matter, so was our own; for, although the firing, for the moment, had nearly ceased, I had not yet clearly made up my mind which side had been the offensive, which the defensive, or which the winning. I had merely the satisfaction of knowing that we had not lost it; for we had met fairly in the middle of a field, (or, rather unfairly, considering that they had two to one,) and, after the scramble was over, our division still held the ground they fought on. All doubts on the subject, however, began to be removed about five o'clock. The enemy's artillery once more opened; and, on running to the brow of the hill, to ascertain the cause, we perceived our old light-division general, Count Alten, at the head of a fresh British division, moving gallantly down the road towards us. It was, indeed, a joyful sight; for, as already mentioned, our division had suffered so severely that we could not help looking forward to a renewal of the action, with such a disparity of force, with considerable anxiety; but this re-inforcement gave us new life, and, as soon as hey came near enough to afford support, we commenced the offensive, and, driving in the skirmishers opposed to us, succeeded in gaining a considerable portion of the position originally occupied by the enemy, when darkness obliged us to desist. In justice to the foreign battalion, which had been all day attached to us, I must say that, in this last movement, they joined us cordially, and behaved exceedingly well. They had a very gallant young fellow at their head; and their conduct, in the earlier part of the day, can, therefore, only be ascribed to its being their first appearance on such a stage.

Leaving General Alten in possession of the ground which we had assisted in winning, we returned in search of our division, and reached them about eleven at night, lying asleep in their glory, on the field where they had fought, which contained many a bloody trace of the day's work.

The firing, on the side of the Prussians, had

altogether ceased before dark, but recommenced, with redoubled fury, about an hour after; and it was then, as we afterwards learnt, that they lost the battle.

We lay down by our arms, near the farm-house already mentioned, in front of Quatre Bras; and the deuce is in it if we were not in good trim for sleeping, seeing that we had been either marching or fighting for twenty-six successive hours.

An hour before daybreak, next morning, a rattling fire of musketry along the whole line of piquets made every one spring to his arms; and we remained looking as fierce as possible until daylight, when each side was seen expecting an attack, while the piquets were blazing at one another without any ostensible cause: it gradually ceased, as the day advanced, and appeared to have been occasioned by a patrole of dragoons getting between the piquets by accident: when firing commences in the dark it is not easily stopped.

June 17th.—As last night's fighting only ceased

with the daylight, the scene, this morning, presented a savage unsettled appearance; the fields
were strewed with the bodies of men, horses,
torn clothing, and shattered cuirasses; and,
though no movements appeared to be going on
on either side, yet, as occasional shots continued
to be exchanged at different points, it kept every
one wide awake. We had the satisfaction of
knowing that the whole of our army had assembled on the hill behind in the course of the
night.

About nine o'clock, we received the news of
Blucher's defeat, and of his retreat to Wavre.
Lord Wellington, therefore, immediately began
to withdraw his army to the position of Waterloo.

Sir Andrew Barnard was ordered to remain as
long as possible with our battalion, to mask the
retreat of the others; and was told, if we were
attacked, that the whole of the British cavalry
were in readiness to advance to our relief. I
had an idea, however, that a single rifle battalion in the midst of ten thousand dragoons,
would come but indifferently off in the event of

a general crash, and was by no means sorry when, between eleven and twelve o'clock, every regiment had got clear off, and we followed, before the enemy had put any thing in motion against us.

After leaving the village of Quatre Bras, and passing through our cavalry, who were formed on each side of the road, we drew up, at the entrance of Genappe. The rain, at that moment, began to descend in torrents, and our men were allowed to shelter themselves in the nearest houses ; but we were obliged to turn out again in the midst of it, in less than five minutes, as we found the French cavalry and ours already exchanging shots, and the latter were falling back to the more favourable ground behind Genappe ; we, therefore, retired with them, *en masse,* through the village, and formed again on the rising ground beyond.

While we remained there, we had an opportunity of seeing the different affairs of cavalry ; and it did ones heart good to see how cordially the life-guards went at their work : they had no idea of any thing but straight-forward fighting, and sent their opponents flying in all directions. The only *young* thing they showed was in every one who got a roll in the mud, (and, owing to the slipperiness of the ground, there were many,) going off to the rear, according to their Hyde-Park custom, as being no longer fit to appear on parade ! I thought, at first, that they had been all wounded, but, on finding how the case stood, I could not help telling them that theirs was now the situation to verify the old proverb, " the uglier the better soldier !"

The roads, as well as the fields, had now become so heavy, that our progress to the rear was very slow ; and it was six in the evening before we drew into the position of Waterloo. Our battalion took post in the second line that night, with its right resting on the Namur-road, behind La Haye Sainte, near a small mud-cottage, which Sir Andrew Barnard occupied as a quarter. The enemy arrived in front, in considerable force, about an hour after us, and a cannonade took place in different parts of the line, which ended at dark, and we lay down by our arms. It rained excessively hard the greater part of the night; nevertheless, having succeeded in getting a bundle of hay for my horse, and one of straw for myself, I secured the horse to his bundle, by tying him to one of the men's swords stuck in the ground, and, placing mine under his nose, I laid myself down upon it, and never opened my eyes again until daylight.

CHAP. XXI.

Battle of Waterloo. " A Horse! a Horse!" Breakfast. Position. Disposition. Meeting of *particular* Friends. Dish of Powder and Ball. Fricassee of Swords. End of First Course. Pounding. Brewing. Peppering. Cutting and Maiming. Fury. Tantalizing. Charging. Cheering. Chasing. Opinionizing. Anecdotes. The End.

BATTLE OF WATERLOO,

18th June, 1815.

WHEN I awoke, this morning, at daylight, I found myself drenched with rain. I had slept so long and so soundly that I had, at first, but a very confused notion of my situation; but having a bright idea that my horse had been my companion when I went to sleep, I was rather startled at finding that I was now alone; nor could I rub my eyes clear enough to procure a sight of him, which was vexatious enough; for, independent of his value *as a horse*, his services were indispensable; and an adjutant might as well think of going into action without his arms as without such a supporter. But whatever my feelings might have been towards him, it was evident that he had none for me, from having drawn his sword and marched off. The chances of finding him again, amid ten thousand others, were about equal to the odds against the needle in a bundle of hay; but for once the single chance was gained, as, after a diligent search of an hour, he was discovered between two artillery horses, about half a mile from where he broke loose.

The weather cleared up as the morning advanced; and, though every thing remained quiet at the moment, we were confident that the day would not pass off without an engagement, and, therefore, proceeded to put our arms in order, as, also, to get ourselves dried and made as comfortable as circumstances would permit.

We made a fire against the wall of Sir Andrew Barnard's cottage, and boiled a huge camp-kettle full of tea, mixed up with a suitable quantity of milk and sugar, for breakfast; and, as it stood on the edge of the high road, where all the big-wigs of the army had occasion to pass, in the early part of the morning, I believe almost every one of them, from the Duke downwards, claimed a cupful.

About nine o'clock, we received an order to retain a quantity of spare ammunition, in some secure place, and to send every thing in the shape of baggage and baggage-animals to the rear. It, therefore, became evident that the Duke meant to give battle in his present position; and it was, at the same time, generally understood that a corps of thirty thousand Prussians were moving to our support.

About ten o'clock, an unusual bustle was observable among the staff-officers, and we soon after received an order to stand to our arms. The troops who had been stationed in our front during the night were then moved off to the right, and our division took up its fighting position.

Our battalion stood on what was considered the left centre of the position. We had our right resting on the Namur-road, about a hundred yards in rear of the farm-house of La Haye Sainte, and our left extending behind a broken hedge, which run along the ridge to the left. Immediately in our front, and divided from La Haye Sainte only by the great road, stood a small knoll, with a sand-hole in its farthest side, which we occupied, as an advanced post, with three companies. The remainder of the division was formed in two lines; the first, consisting chiefly of light troops, behind the hedge, in continuation from the left of our battalion reserve; and the second, about a hundred yards in its rear. The guns were placed in the intervals between the brigades, two pieces were in the road-way on our right, and a rocket-brigade in the centre.

The road had been cut through the rising ground, and was about twenty or thirty feet deep where our right rested, and which, in a manner, separated us from all the troops beyond. The division, I believe, under General Alten occupied the ground next to us, on the right. He had a light battalion of the German legion, posted inside of La Haye Sainte, and the household brigade of cavalry stood under cover of the rising ground behind him. On our left there were some Hanoverians and Belgians, together with a brigade of British heavy dragoons, the royals, and Scotch greys.

These were all the observations on the disposition of our army that my situation enabled me to make. The whole position seemed to be a gently rising ground, presenting no obstacle at any point, excepting the broken hedge in front of our division, and it was only one in appearance, as it could be passed in every part.

Shortly after we had taken up our ground, some columns, from the enemy's left, were seen in motion towards Hugamont, and were soon warmly engaged with the right of our army. A cannon ball, too, came from the Lord knows where, for it was not fired at us, and took the head off our right hand man. That part of their position, in our own immediate front, next claimed our undivided attention. It had hitherto been looking suspiciously innocent, with scarcely a human being upon it; but innumerable black specks were now seen taking post at regular distances in its front, and recognizing them as so many pieces of artillery, I knew, from experience, although nothing else was yet visible, that they were unerring symptoms of our not being destined to be idle spectators.

From the moment we took possession of the knoll, we had busied ourselves in collecting branches of trees and other things, for the purpose of making an *abatis* to block up the road between that and the farm-house, and soon completed one, which we thought looked sufficiently formidable to keep out the whole of the French cavalry; but it was put to the proof sooner than we expected, by a troop of our own light dragoons, who, having occasion to gallop through, astonished us not a little by clearing away every stick of it. We had just time to replace the scattered branches, when the whole of the enemy's artillery opened, and their countless columns began to advance under cover of it.

The scene at that moment was grand and imposing, and we had a few minutes to spare for observation. The column destined as *our* particular *friends,* first attracted our notice, and seemed to consist of about ten thousand infantry. A smaller body of infantry and one of cavalry moved on their right; and, on their left, another huge column of infantry, and a formidable body of cuirassiers, while beyond them it seemed one moving mass.

We saw Buonaparte himself take post on the side of the road, immediately in our front, surrounded by a numerous staff; and each regiment, as they passed him, rent the air with shouts of " *vive l'Empereur,*" nor did they cease after they had passed; but, backed by the thunder of their artillery, and carrying with them the *rubidub* of drums, and the *tantarara* of trumpets, in addition to their increasing shouts, it

looked, at first, as if they had some hopes of
scaring us off the ground; for it was a singular
contrast to the stern silence reigning on our
side, where nothing, as yet, but the voices of
our great guns, told that we had mouths to
open when we chose to use them.   Our rifles
were, however, in a very few seconds, required
to play their parts, and opened such a fire on
the advancing skirmishers as quickly brought
them to a stand still; but their columns advanced steadily through them, although our incessant *tiralade* was telling in their centre with
fearful exactness, and our post was quickly
turned in both flanks, which compelled us to
fall back and join our comrades, behind the
hedge, though not before some of our officers
and theirs had been engaged in personal
combat.

When the heads of their columns shewed over
the knoll which we had just quitted, they received such a fire from our first line, that they
wavered, and hung behind it a little; but, cheered
and encouraged by the gallantry of their officers,

who were dancing and flourishing their swords in front, they at last boldly advanced to the opposite side of our hedge, and began to deploy. Our first line, in the mean time, was getting so thinned, 'that Picton found it necessary to bring up his second, but fell in the act of doing it. The command of the division, at that critical moment, devolved upon Sir James Kempt, who was galloping along the line, animating the men to steadiness. He called to me by name, where I happened to be standing on the right of our battalion, and desired " that I would never " quit that spot." I told him that " he might " depend upon it :" and in another instant I found myself in a fair way of keeping my promise more religiously than I intended; for, glancing my eye to the right, I saw the next field covered with the cuirassiers, some of whom were making directly for the gap in the hedge, where I was standing. I had not hitherto drawn my sword, as it was generally to be had at a moment's warning; but, from its having been exposed to the last night's rain, it had now got

rusted in the scabbard, and refused to come
forth! I was in a precious scrape. Mounted on
my strong Flanders mare, and with my good
old sword in my hand, I would have braved all
the chances without a moment's hesitation; but,
I confess, that I felt considerable doubts as to
the propriety of standing there to be sacrificed,
without the means of making a scramble for it.
My mind, however, was happily relieved from
such an embarrassing consideration, before my
decision was required; for the next moment the
cuirassiers were charged by our household brigade; and the infantry in our front giving way
at the same time, under our terrific shower of
musketry, the flying cuirassiers tumbled in
among the routed infantry, followed by the life-
guards, who were cutting away in all directions.
Hundreds of the infantry threw themselves down,
and pretended to be dead, while the cavalry
galloped over them, and then got up and ran
away. I never saw such a scene in all my life.

Lord Wellington had given orders that the
troops were, on no account, to leave the position

to follow up any temporary advantage ; so that we now resumed our post, as we stood at the commencement of the battle, and with three companies again advanced on the knoll.

I was told, it was very ridiculous, at that moment, to see the number of vacant spots that were left nearly along the whole of the line, where a great part of the dark dressed foreign troops had stood, intermixed with the British, when the action began.

Our division got considerably reduced in numbers during the last attack ; but Lord Wellington's fostering hand sent Sir John Lambert to our support, with the sixth division ; and we now stood prepared for another and a more desperate struggle.

Our battalion had already lost three officers killed, and six or seven wounded; among the latter were Sir Andrew Barnard and Colonel Cameron.

Some one asking me what had become of my horse's ear, was the first intimation I had of his being wounded ; and I now found that, inde-

Q

pendent of one ear having been shaved close to his head, (I suppose by a cannon-shot,) a musket-ball had grazed across his forehead, and another gone through one of his legs, but he did not seem much the worse for either of them.

Between two and three o'clock we were tolerably quiet, except from a thundering cannonade; and the enemy had, by that time, got the range of our position so accurately that every shot brought a ticket for somebody's head.

An occasional gun, beyond the plain, far to our left, marked the approach of the Prussians; but their progress was too slow to afford a hope of their arriving in time to take any share in the battle.

On our right, the roar of cannon and musketry had been incessant from the time of its commencement; but the higher ground, near us, prevented our seeing anything of what was going on.

Between three and four o'clock, the storm gathered again in our front. Our three companies on the knoll were soon involved in a furious fire. The Germans, occupying La Haye Sainte, expended all their ammunition, and fled from the post. The French took possession of it; and, as it flanked our knoll, we were obliged to abandon it also, and fall back again behind the hedge.

The loss of La Haye Sainte was of the most serious consequence, as it afforded the enemy an establishment within our position. They immediately brought up two guns on our side of it, and began serving out some grape to us; but they were so very near, that we destroyed their artillerymen before they could give us a second round.

The silencing of these guns was succeeded by a very extraordinary scene, on the same spot. A strong regiment of Hanoverians advanced in line, to charge the enemy out of La Haye Sainte; but they were themselves charged by a brigade of cuirassiers, and, excepting one officer, on a little black horse, who went off to the rear, like a shot out of a shovel, I do believe that every man of them was put to death in about five seconds. A brigade of British light dragoons advanced to their relief, and a few, on each side, began exchanging thrusts; but it seemed likely to be a drawn battle between them, without much harm being done, when our men brought it to a crisis sooner than either side anticipated, for they previously had their rifles eagerly pointed at the cuirassiers, with a view of saving the perishing Hanoverians; but the fear of killing their friends withheld them, until the others were utterly overwhelmed, when they instantly opened a terrific fire on the whole concern, sending both sides to flight; so that, on the small space of ground, within a hundred yards of us, where five thousand men had been fighting the instant before, there was not now a living soul to be seen.

It made me mad to see the cuirassiers, in their retreat, stooping and stabbing at our wounded men, as they lay on the ground. How

I wished that I had been blessed with Omnipotent power for a moment, that I might have blighted them!

The same field continued to be a wild one the whole of the afternoon. It was a sort of duelling-post between the two armies, every half-hour showing a meeting of some kind upon it; but they never exceeded a short scramble, for men's lives were held very cheap there.

For the two or three succeeding hours there was no variety with us, but one continued blaze of musketry. The smoke hung so thick about, that, although not more than eighty yards asunder, we could only distinguish each other by the flashes of the pieces.

A good many of our guns had been disabled, and a great many more rendered unserviceable in consequence of the unprecedented close fighting; for, in several places, where they had been posted but a very few yards in front of the line, it was impossible to work them.

I shall never forget the scene which the field of battle presented about seven in the evening.

I felt weary and worn out, less from fatigue than anxiety. Our division, which had stood upwards of five thousand men at the commencement of the battle, had gradually dwindled down into a solitary line of skirmishers. The twenty-seventh regiment were lying literally dead, in square, a few yards behind us. My horse had received another shot through the leg, and one through the flap of the saddle, which lodged in his body, sending him a step beyond the pension-list. The smoke still hung so thick about us that we could see nothing. I walked a little way to each flank, to endeavour to get a glimpse of what was going on; but nothing met my eye except the mangled remains of men and horses, and I was obliged to return to my post as wise as I went.

I had never yet heard of a battle in which every body was killed ; but this seemed likely to be an exception, as all were going by turns. We got excessively impatient under the tame similitude of the latter part of the process, and burned with desire to have a last thrust at our respective *vis-à-vis* ; for, however desperate our affairs were, we had still the satisfaction of seeing that theirs were worse. Sir John Lambert continued to stand as our support, at the head of three good old regiments, one dead (the twenty-seventh) and two living ones ; and we took the liberty of soliciting him to aid our views ; but the Duke's orders on that head were so very particular that the gallant general had no choice.

Presently a cheer, which we knew to be British, commenced far to the right, and made every one prick up his ears ;—it was Lord Wellington's long wished-for orders to advance ; it gradually approached, growing louder as it grew near;—we took it up by instinct, charged through the hedge down upon the old knoll, sending our adversaries flying at the point of the bayonet. Lord Wellington galloped up to us at the instant, and our men began to cheer him ; but he called out, " no cheering, my lads, but forward, and complete your victory !"

This movement had carried us clear of the

smoke ; and, to people who had been for so many hours enveloped in darkness, in the midst of destruction, and naturally anxious about the result of the day, the scene which now met the eye conveyed a feeling of more exquisite gratification than can be conceived. It was a fine summer's evening, just before sunset. The French were flying in one confused mass. British lines were seen in close pursuit, and in admirable order, as far as the eye could reach to the right, while the plain to the left was filled with Prussians. The enemy made one last attempt at a stand on the rising ground to our right of La Belle Alliance ; but a charge from General Adams's brigade again threw them into a state of confusion, which was now inextricable, and their ruin was complete. Artillery, baggage, and every thing belonging to them, fell into our hands. After pursuing them until dark, we halted about two miles beyond the field of battle, leaving the Prussians to follow up the victory.

This was the last, the greatest, and the most uncomfortable heap of glory that I ever had a hand in, and may the deuce take me if I think that every body waited there to see the end of it, otherwise it never could have been so troublesome to those who did. We were, take us all in all, a very bad army. Our foreign auxiliaries, who constituted more than half of our numerical strength, with some exceptions, were little better than a raw militia—a body without a soul, or like an inflated pillow, that gives to the touch, and resumes its shape again when the pressure ceases—not to mention the many who went clear out of the field, and were only seen while plundering our baggage in their retreat.

Our heavy cavalry made some brilliant charges in the early part of the day; but they never knew when to stop, their ardour in following their advantages carrying them headlong on, until many of them " burnt their fingers," and got dispersed or destroyed.

Of that gallant corps, the royal artillery, it is enough to say, that they maintained their former reputation—the first in the world—and it was a serious loss to us, in the latter part of the day, to be deprived of this more powerful co-operation, from the causes already mentioned.

The British infantry and the King's German legion continued the inflexible supporters of their country's honour throughout, and their un-shaken constancy under the most desperate cir-cumstances showed that, though they might be destroyed, they were not to be beaten.

If Lord Wellington had been at the head of his old Peninsula army, I am confident that he would have swept his opponents off the face of the earth immediately after their first attack ; but with such a heterogeneous mixture under his command, he was obliged to submit to a longer day.

It will ever be a matter of dispute what the result of that day would have been without the arrival of the Prussians : but it is clear to me that Lord Wellington would not have fought at Waterloo unless Blucher had promised to aid him with 30,000 men, as he required that number to put him on a numerical footing with his adversary. It is certain that the promised aid did not come in time to take any share whatever in the battle. It is equally certain that the enemy had, long before, been beaten into a mass of ruin, in condition for nothing but running, and wanting but an apology to do it; and I will ever maintain that Lord Wellington's last advance would have made it the same victory had a Prussian never been seen there.

The field of battle, next morning, presented a frightful scene of carnage; it seemed as if the world had tumbled to pieces, and three-fourths of every thing destroyed in the wreck. The ground running parallel to the front of where we had stood was so thickly strewed with fallen men and horses, that it was difficult to step clear of their bodies; many of the former still alive, and imploring assistance, which it was not in our power to bestow.

The usual salutation on meeting an acquaintance of another regiment after an action was to

ask who had been hit? but on this occasion it
was "Who's alive?" Meeting one, next morning, a very little fellow, I asked what had
happened to them yesterday? "I'll be hanged,"
says he, "if I know any thing at all about the
matter, for I was all day trodden in the mud
and galloped over by every scoundrel who had
a horse; and, in short, that I only owe my
existence to my insignificance."

Two of our men, on the morning of the 19th,
lost their lives by a very melancholy accident.
They were cutting up a captured ammunition-
waggon for firewood, when one of their swords
striking against a nail, sent a spark among the
powder. When I looked in the direction of
the explosion, I saw the two poor fellows about
twenty or thirty feet up in the air. On falling to
the ground, though lying on their backs or
bellies, some extraordinary effort of nature,
caused by the agony of the moment, made
them spring from that position, five or six times,
to the height of eight or ten feet, just as a fish

does when thrown on the ground after being newly caught. It was so unlike a scene in real life that it was impossible to witness it without forgetting, for a moment, the horror of their situation.

I ran to the spot along with others, and found that every stitch of clothes had been burnt off, and they were black as ink all over. They were still alive, and told us their names, otherwise we could not have recognized them; and, singular enough, they were able to walk off the ground with a little support, but died shortly after.

Among other officers who fell at Waterloo, we lost one of the wildest youths that ever belonged to the service. He seemed to have a prophetic notion of his approaching end, for he repeatedly told us, in the early part of the morning, that he knew the devil would have him before night. I shall relate one anecdote of him, which occurred while we were in Spain. He went, by chance, to pass the day with two officers, quartered at a neighbouring village, who happened to be, that day, engaged to dine with the clergyman. Knowing their visitor's mischievous propensities, they were at first afraid to make him one of the party; but, after schooling him into a suitable propriety of behaviour, and exacting a promise of implicit obedience, they, at last, ventured to take him. On their arrival, the ceremony of introduction had just been gone through, and their host seated at an open window, when a favourite cat of his went purring about the young gentleman's boots, who, catching it by the tail, and giving it two or three preparatory swings round his head, sent it flying out at the window where the parson was sitting, who only escaped it by suddenly stooping. The only apology the youngster made for his conduct was, "Egad, I think I astonished that fellow!" but whether it was the cat or the parson he meant I never could learn.

About twelve o'clock, on the day after the

battle, we commenced our march for Paris. I shall, therefore, leave my readers at Waterloo, in the hope that, among the many stories of romance to which that and the other celebrated fields gave birth, the foregoing unsophisticated one of an eye-witness may not have been found altogether uninteresting.

THE END.

ERRATA.

Page 7, line 13, *read* " of lively."

Page 9, line 18, *read* " reinforced" *instead of* " reenforced."

Page 25, line 17, *read* " her's" *instead of* " hers."

Page 27, line 3, *read* " with him!!!"

Page 73, line 8, *read* " when we" *instead of* " when it."

Page 154, line 21, *read* " 17th" *instead of* " 19th."

Page 178, line 14, *read* " re-crossed" *instead of* " re-crosed."

Page 219, line 17, *read* " held one side" *instead of* " held on one side."

Page 266, line 13, *read* " dying state ;" *instead of* " dying; state."

Page 269, lines 14 and 15, *read* " to remark in a French officer, occurred" *instead of* " to remark was that of a French officer, which occurred."

"Among the publications which we have lately perused with pleasure, are the two volumes of Colonel Napier's *History of the War in the Peninsula*, which, so far as the author has conducted his work, convey an interesting record of a series of glorious military events, as remarkable for their variety and important results, as for the spirit and constancy with which they were maintained, and the valour and heroism which marked their execution.

"Colonel Napier shared in the glory of the Peninsular campaigns, and besides being a competent eye-witness of the chief events which he relates, he appears to have had, both from the Duke of Wellington and Marshal Soult, peculiar sources of information respecting the military movements of these great soldiers."—*Times.*

"The narrative is very circumstantial, and Colonel Napier appears to have been very diligent in his researches. The facilities afforded him by a state of peace have enabled him to examine documents from French as well as British officers—The papers of Marshal Soult, and of his less able colleague, Marshal Jourdan, being referred to on several occasions of importance.

"This book, if not of much interest to those who read for amusement, will be found to possess great attractions to military readers, and to those who are disposed to study history with attention, analyzing the cause of extraordinary events, and marking the different traits of character which belongs to generals and ministers. The commanders who figure most conspicuously in the present volume, are Lord Wellington and Marshal Soult ; but there are occasional references of interest to other eminent actors on the scene of operations in the Peninsula, in particular to Napoleon and Sir John Moore."—*Courier.*

"If the legitimate province of history be, as we have always understood it, to put clearly on record the facts of which it treats as far as they can be ascertained, free from the colouring or bias of either party views or personal prejudices, this book of Colonel Napier's is, indeed, a model of a historical work. It should be borne in mind, that the work of Colonel Napier is a book, *not merely for the present day, but for all time.*"—*Liverpool Chronicle.*

"Il y a long-tems qu'on sent en Angleterre le besoin d'un ouvrage militaire classique propre à guider la jeunesse, et à l'initier du métier des armes. Ce vide dans la littérature des camps, va se trouver rempli par le livre de M. le Col. Napier. Il deviendra le compagnon de l'officier comme du soldat, il doit trouver place dans la giberne comme dans le portmanteau. Il sera lu sous la tente et dans la caserne ; d'une utilité universelle, il doit conséquement figurer sur le premier rayon de toute bibliothèque militaire."— *Le Furet de Londres.*

SUPPLEMENT to an INQUIRY into the INTEGRITY of the GREEK VULGATE, or Received Text of the New Testament; containing the Vindication of the Principles employed in its Defence. By the Rev. FREDERICK NOLAN, LL.D. F.R.L.S. Vicar of Prittlewell, Essex. 1 Vol. 8vo. boards, price 8s.

BY THE SAME AUTHOR.

A HARMONICAL GRAMMAR of the Latin Language. 8vo. sewed, price 4s.
Ditto of the French. 8vo. price 4s.
Ditto of the Italian. 8vo. price 4s.
Ditto of the Spanish. 8vo. price 4s.
Printed verbatim from a Harmonical Grammar of the principal ancient

Published and sold by T. & W. BOONE, 480, *Strand, near Charing-Cross.*

and modern languages. Each language is treated upon *a uniform plan*, and analyzed on new and simple principles; short and comprehensive rules are given, for attaining a just pronunciation, for determining the gender, and inflecting the noun and verb,—together with a Syntax and Prosody, fully exemplified, and a classed vocabulary of the most useful and necessary words.

The EXPECTATIONS FORMED BY THE ASSYRIANS, THAT A GREAT DELIVERER WOULD APPEAR, ABOUT THE TIME OF OUR LORD'S ADVENT, DEMONSTRATED. 8vo. price 10*s.* boards.
And all the other Works of the same Author.

TRACTS ON VAULTS AND BRIDGES; containing Observations on the various Forms of Vaults; on the Taking Down and Rebuilding LONDON BRIDGE; and on the PRINCIPLES of ARCHES: illustrated by extensive Tables of Bridges. Also, containing the Principles of PENDANT BRIDGES, with reference to the Properties of the Catenary, applied to the Menai Bridge. And a Theoretical Investigation of the Catenary. By SAMUEL WARE. With 20 copper-plates and 10 wood-cuts, royal 8vo. price 20*s.* boards.
This Book will be found of the highest importance to Military as well as Civil Engineers, being the only practical work on the subject of Suspension Bridges.

BY THE SAME AUTHOR.
A DESIGN FOR A TUNNEL UNDER THE THAMES, from Horsely-down to St. Katharine's, with Letter-press Description. Price 3*s.*

ALSO, BY THE SAME AUTHOR.
REMARKS ON THEATRES; and on the Propriety of *Vaulting them with Brick and Stone*: with Observations on the CONSTRUCTION OF DOMES; and the Vaults of the Free and Accepted Masons. With 3 copper-plates, royal 8vo. sewed, price 6*s.*

An HISTORICAL AND DESCRIPTIVE ACCOUNT OF THE SUSPEN-SION BDIDGE constructed over the *Menai Strait*, in North Wales; with a brief Notice of CONWAY BRIDGE. From Designs by, and under the direction of THOMAS TELFORD. By WILLIAM ALEXANDER PROVIS, the Resident-Engineer. *With Elevations, Sections, and Details, on a very large scale.* Atlas folio, boards, 7*l.* 7*s.*

PORTRAITS OF THE WORTHIES OF WESTMINSTER HALL, with their AUTOGRAPHS; being Fac-similes of Original Sketches, found in the Note-Book of a BRIEFLESS BARRISTER. Part I. 8vo. containing Portraits of

The Lord Chancellor.	Philip Courtney, Esq.
Lord Tenterden.	Thomas Starkie, Esq.
Sir John Bayley.	James Parke, Esq.
Jonathan Raine, Esq. M.P.	James Browne, Esq.
Sir James Scarlett, M.P.	Henry Lawrence, Esq.
John Gurney, Esq.	Benjamin Rotch, Esq.
Frederick Pollock, Esq.	John Patteson, Esq.
John Williams, Esq. M.P.	Henry Raper, Esq.
Henry Brougham, Esq. M.P.	William Whateley, Esq.
Richard Ashworth, Esq.	

Coloured, price 20*s.*

Part II. is preparing, for which the publishers will be obliged by receiving subscriber's names.

Published and sold by T. & W. BOONE, 480, *Strand, near Charing-Cross.*

OUTLINES OF THE GEOLOGY OF ENGLAND AND WALES ; with an introductory Compendium of the general Principles of that Science, and comparative Views of the Structure of FOREIGN COUNTRIES. Illustrated by a *coloured map* and sections, &c. By the Rev. W. D. CONYBAERE, and W. PHILLIPS, 8vo. part 1, boards, 16s.

" We do not hesitate to pronounce this to be the best Geological Work extant; it presents the reader with a perspicuous statement of the uses and objects of Geology, with a detailed and skilful account of the Geology of England ; and with much minute and practical information upon a variety of important subjects connected with the applications of the branch of Science of which it treats."—*Brande's Journal.*

PORTRAIT OF THE LATE MAURICE BIRKBECK, Esq. of the Illanois, with his AUTOGRAPH, in Lithography, sketched, by a Friend, previous to his last Voyage to America Price 2s.

A TREATISE ON THE GAME OF WHIST, by the late Admiral CHARLES BURNEY, Author of Voyages and Discoveries in the Pacific, &c. *Second Edition.* 18mo. boards. Price 2s.

" The kind of play recommended in this Treatise is on the most plain, and what the Author considers the most safe principles. I have limited my endeavours to the most necessary instructions, classing them as much as the subject enabled me, under separate heads, to facilitate their being rightly comprehended and easily remembered. For the greater encouragement of the learner, I have studied brevity ; but not in a degree to have prevented my endeavouring more to make the principles of the game, and the rationality of them, intelligible, than to furnish a young player with a set of rules to get by rote, that he might go blindly right."

TRANSACTIONS OF THE MEDICO-BOTANICAL SOCIETY OF LONDON ; containing, with other Papers, an Account of the ANGUSTURA BARK TREE. Vol. I. Part I. 8vo. plates, price 6s.

A New Edition of WITHERING'S SYSTEMATIC ARRANGEMENT OF BRITISH PLANTS, much enlarged and improved. *Just ready.*

‾ Part I. and II. (to be had *gratis*) of a Catalogue of Books on English and Irish History, the Fine Arts, Classics, &c. &c., in fine condition, now on sale, by T. and W. BOONE.

LONDON:

MARCHANT, PRINTER, INGRAM-COURT.

Also published in facsimile in **The Spellmount Library of Military History** and available from all good bookshops:

RANDOM SHOTS FROM A RIFLEMAN by Captain John Kincaid
Introduction by Ian Fletcher

Originally published in 1835, this was the author's follow-up to *Adventures in the Rifle Brigade* – and is a collection of highly amusing, entertaining and informative anecdotes set against the background of the Peninsular War and Waterloo campaign.

RECOLLECTIONS OF THE PENINSULA by Moyle Sherer
Introduction by Philip Haythornthwaite

Reissued more than 170 years after its first publication, this is one of the acknowledged classic accounts of the Peninsular War. Moyle Sherer, described by a comrade as 'a gentleman, a scholar, an author and a most zealous soldier', had a keen eye for observation and an ability to describe both the battles – Busaco, Albuera, Arroyo dos Molinos, Vittoria and the Pyrenees – and the emotions he felt at the time with uncommon clarity.

ROUGH NOTES OF SEVEN CAMPAIGNS: in Portugal, Spain, France and America during the Years 1809–1815 by John Spencer Cooper
Introduction by Jan Fletcher

Originally published in 1869, this is one of the most sought-after volumes of Peninsular War reminiscences. A vivid account of the greatest battles and sieges of the war including Talavera, Busaco, Albuera, Ciudad Rodrigo, Badajoz, Vittoria, the Pyrenees, Orthes and Toulouse and the New Orleans campaign of 1815.

THE MILITARY ADVENTURES OF CHARLES O'NEIL by Charles O'Neil
Introduction by Bernard Cornwell

First published in 1851, these are the memoirs of an Irish soldier who served with Wellington's Army during the Peninsular War and the continental campaigns from 1811 to 1815. Almost unknown in the UK, as the author emigrated to America straight after, it includes his eye-witness accounts of the bloody battle of

Barossa, the memorable siege of Badajoz – and a graphic description of the Battle of Waterloo where he was badly wounded.

MEMOIRS OF THE LATE MAJOR-GENERAL LE MARCHANT
by Denis Le Marchant
Introduction by Nicholas Leadbetter   Foreword by Dr David Chandler

Only 93 copies of the memoirs of the founder of what is now the RMA Sandhurst were published by his son Denis in 1812. His death at Salamanca in 1841 meant that Britain was robbed of its most forward-thinking officer. This facsimile edition is enhanced with additional watercolour pictures by Le Marchant himself.

THE JOURNAL OF AN ARMY SURGEON DURING THE PENINSULAR WAR by Charles Boutflower
Introduction by Dr Christopher Ticehurst

A facsimile edition of a rare journal written by an army surgeon who joined the 40th Regiment in Malta in 1801 and subsequently served with it in the West Indies, South America and the Peninsular War. Described by his family 'as a man of great activity and a general favourite with all his acquaintances', he saw action from 1810 to 1813 including Busaco, Ciudad Rodrigo, Badajoz and Salamanca – gaining a well-deserved promotion to Surgeon to the staff of Sir Rowland Hill's Brigade in 1812.

For a free catalogue, telephone Spellmount Publishers on

01580 893730

or write to

The Old Rectory
Staplehurst
Kent TN12 0AZ
United Kingdom
(Facsimile 01580 893731)